Falling into Grace

EXPLORING OUR INNER LIFE WITH GOD

Falling into Grace

EXPLORING OUR INNER LIFE WITH GOD

John Newton

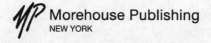

Morehouse Publishing
NEW YORK

Morehouse Publishing, 19 East 34th Street, New York, NY 10016

Morehouse Publishing is an imprint of Church Publishing Incorporated.
www.churchpublishing.org

Cover design by Jennifer Kopec, 2Pug Design
Typeset by Rose Design

Library of Congress Cataloging-in-Publication Data

Names: Newton, John (Canon), author.
Title: Falling into grace : exploring our inner life with God / John Newton.
Description: New York : Morehouse Publishing, 2016. | Includes
  bibliographical references.
Identifiers: LCCN 2015047819 (print) | LCCN 2015050019 (ebook) | ISBN
  9780819232618 (pbk.) | ISBN 9780819232625 (ebook)
Subjects: LCSH: Spiritual life—Christianity. | Spirituality—Christianity. |
  Grace (Theology)
Classification: LCC BV4501.3 .N49 2016 (print) | LCC BV4501.3 (ebook) | DDC
  248.4—dc23
LC record available at http://lccn.loc.gov/2015047819

Printed in the United States of America

To my family

Contents

Acknowledgments

I did not have the capacity to write this book two years ago. My thinking on the nature of the spiritual life continues to evolve, and I find myself deeply grateful for the many teachers, authors, mentors, and encouragers that continue to lead me deeper into the mystery of life in Christ. I wrote this book standing on the shoulders of far too many people to name.

I want to thank Sharon Pearson and the team at Church Publishing for believing in me and in this book. It humbles me to think that someone deems my thoughts worthy of being published. I also want to thank Patrick Hall for reading the first draft of this manuscript. Your invaluable feedback has made this a stronger book.

I would also like to express my deep gratitude for the Episcopal Diocese of Texas. I am blessed to work with incredibly gifted and passionate clergy and laity week in and week out. *Falling into Grace* is the natural outgrowth of sharing with you in God's mission.

Finally, I want to thank my family and friends, and especially my wife, Emily, and my daughter, Annie. I am incredibly blessed to have each one of you in my life. You make life beautiful.

Introduction

There's a story about a beggar who had been panhandling by the road for most of his life. On one particular day a stranger walked by. "Spare a little change?" mumbled the beggar. "I have no money," replied the stranger, "but what's that you are you sitting on?" "Nothing," replied the beggar. "It's just an old box. I've been sitting on it for as long as I can remember." "Have you ever looked inside?" asked the stranger. "No," muttered the beggar. "What's the point? There's nothing in there." "Open the box and have a look inside," the stranger insisted. Though reluctant, the beggar managed to pry open the lid and with astonishment and joy he saw that his box was filled with gold.[1]

It's an intriguing thought, isn't it? That one could be rich and mistake him or herself to be a poor beggar? I wonder if the same could be true about us.

I know that life rarely feels like we're sitting on gold. It *feels* like we're sitting on deadlines, demands, routines, disappointments, complex relationships, dirty diapers, existential angst, and a nagging sense that there just isn't "enough" to go around—enough time, enough money, enough energy, enough of a connection to God or to our church—enough *anything*. Life has a funny way of making us feel like the box is empty.

I often marvel why this should be so and I've concluded that our all-pervading sense of scarcity stems from the fact that most of us are zealously committed to a lie. Our hearts are all too eager to deny what the Bible emphatically proclaims as world-altering news: namely, that the universe and every aspect of our life *has already been reconciled to God* (see 2 Cor. 5:19). To put it a bit differently, we are home free before the game even starts. We live on earth as adopted sons and daughters of God, "possessing everything" as Paul put it. The great task of the spiritual life isn't so much to go anywhere or do anything, but rather to wake up, celebrate, and "see" ourselves and one another in a different Light.

Falling into Grace is an invitation to open the box of your life and to have a look inside. I write from a deep conviction that every aspect of this world has been reconciled with God in the life, death, and resurrection of Jesus Christ and that, regardless of what we feel on any given day, God's grace permeates our life right down to the smallest detail. However, rather than being a mere comfort and support, I believe God's grace to be deeply threatening to the life that we have constructed. Grace is not some spiritual vitamin we take that helps us control our life, but the all-consuming experience of God's Life taking over, which *always* leaves us more relinquished to God than before. It is an experience that feels an awful lot like falling. Like Jacob, we limp away from the encounter with God not quite sure what happened or what to make of the experience.

There is nothing inside of us that instinctively wants to fall, even though Jesus routinely told us that he came, not to teach us how to succeed, but rather how to fall, lose, and die. We run from the experience of falling because we forget that resurrection always awaits us on the other side of death. We only experience healing, find our purpose, engage our suffering differently, evangelize the world more gracefully, and wake up to see ourselves as already resurrected *in* the falling.

This book is an invitation to let yourself fall. It's a reminder that, because you're already home free from the beginning, any fall can always be a fall into grace. And so don't expect to find within these pages a list of spiritual exercises that will help you grow closer to God. Growing closer to God is impossible. It's like saying that you want to grow closer to your skin. What actually "grows" is our subtle sense of union with God; in reality God has always been and will always be much closer to us than we are to ourselves. We are not solitary pilgrims looking to the heavens and calling out *to* God, but adopted sons and daughters looking out at the world, each other, and ourselves *through* God. "For '*In Him* we live and move and have our being'" (Acts 17:28, italics mine). We are already "in" Christ. We need not ascend but fall deeper into an awareness of that experience.

There's an old story about a disciple and his teacher. "Where shall I find God?" a disciple once asked. "Here," the teacher said. "Then why can't I see God?" "Because you do not look." "Well, what should I look for?" "Nothing, just look," responded the teacher. "But at what?" "Anything your eyes alight upon," the teacher said. "But must I look in a special sort of way?" "No," said the teacher, "The ordinary way will do." "But don't I always look in the ordinary way?" "No, you don't," the teacher replied. "Because to look, you must be *here*. But you're mostly somewhere else."[2]

As you begin reading this book, I wonder: where have you been looking for God? In God you live, move, and have your being—*right now*. You are not a beggar at all, but in fact wealthier than you could ever dare dream.

Open your life and have a look inside. Right now. Right *here*. You might just discover that the box is filled with gold.

1

Grace

"The American Church today accepts grace in theory but denies it in practice." —*Brennan Manning*

"Amazing Grace, how sweet the sound, that saved a wretch like me. I once was lost but now am found, was blind, but now I see." —*John Newton*

"For judgment I came into this world, that those who do not see may see, and those who see may become blind." —*John 9:39 (ESV)*

The month after I graduated from college I went with a church group to build a house in Tijuana, Mexico. After our work was completed, we spent a day at Disneyland before flying back home. During the trip I lost my contact lenses to the dusty, Mexican desert. I could not see a thing. I had my glasses with me but was too stubborn to admit that I actually needed them to navigate the Magic Kingdom.

Around lunchtime I thought I saw a fruit stand that flaunted the most gorgeous bananas I'd ever seen. They looked freshly plucked from the Garden of Eden. With enthusiasm I approached the young lady working the stand, "One banana, please!" "That will be four dollars," she replied. A little steep, I thought, but still a small price to pay for perfection.

I handed her my money and reached for a banana only to find that the banana would not cooperate. I wanted the banana, but it was as if the banana did not want me. I tugged and tugged but could not break a banana free from the bunch.

I then noticed the woman laughing at me. "Perhaps you'd like one of these," she giggled, as she pointed to a much more inferior batch of fruit. "I don't think so," I said. "Well, I don't think the bananas you're holding will taste very good," she replied. "And why is that?" I sneered back. "Because the bananas you're holding are fake."

I obviously felt embarrassed. So I covered my tracks by doing what I suspect any aspiring minister would do. I looked exactly eight inches to her left, opened my eyelids as wide as I could, and, before dramatically storming off in anger, responded by saying, "I am *soooo* sorry ma'am. I can't help it. I'm legally blind."

Born Blind

In a spiritual sense we are all born blind. Our default state is not to see God, ourselves, and other people accurately. We're programmed to stumble through life in darkness, and the pathos of our condition is that it is painful to constantly collide with one another.

The gospels portray Jesus as a man who loved healing people's blindness. The author of John's Gospel tells one such story about blind people. It centers on a man who has been without physical sight from the day of his birth (John 9:1–41). But the irony of the story is that no one with physical sight possesses the spiritual sight they need to see

God, themselves, or other people accurately. The people in the story that can "see" are indeed blinder than the blind man himself. For instance, the disciples assume the man was born blind because his parents are sinners. They are blind to the goodness of God. Similarly, the man's parents care more for their reputation than their own son. They are blind to what's important in life. The Pharisees feel outraged because Jesus heals on the Sabbath. The Pharisees care more about rules than restoration. They are blind to the Christ that stands before them. Meanwhile Jesus, who sees into the soul with crystal clarity, responds by stating His divine purpose: "For judgment I came into this world, that those who do not see may see, and those who see may become blind" (John 9:39, ESV).

Subverting Our Paradigm

I saw a bumper sticker recently that read: "Subvert the dominant paradigm." It made me realize why people responded to Jesus with so much hostility. It was because Jesus intentionally subverted their view of God and how the world should work. Jesus was a wrecking ball, and his first order of business was never to confirm his listener's view of the world, but rather to shatter it.

The word *paradigm* has Greek origins and refers to how we see, and therefore experience, the world. Our paradigms are our mental maps of the world. We don't experience the world directly, but we have mental maps we rely on to navigate the world. We don't just perceive, understand, and interpret life as it comes. Rather, we have a very particular frame of reference that we use to make meaning out of the people, circumstances, and events that we encounter. We all carry unconscious assumptions about God's character, how the world works, and what abundant life is all about.

What's challenging about the spiritual life is that we don't *see* our paradigms, at least not naturally. We inherit them. Life, religion, the government, our family, the culture, our church, the media, and our peers just dole them out. For example, I was raised in the western United States. My paradigm for living well is certainly more individualistic than had I been reared in a traditional Asian culture. I am also a Protestant. I carry ingrained views about what sort of behavior is acceptable that a person practicing Wicca, for example, might not have. But I am also a particular kind of Protestant. I grew up in a very traditional, liturgical church setting with pews, an organ, and prayer books. I see God differently than someone that grew up in a contemporary, Pentecostal setting.

We all have a unique mental map, and this map is never the same as the real world. A mental map is what we use to *navigate* the real world. It is the lens through which we view God, ourselves, and other people. In the spiritual life, it is this lens, this mental map, which so heavily impacts our experience of God, ourselves, and other people. A distorted lens always leads to a distorted life, and to navigate with a bad map is to live our lives perpetually lost.

Sociologist Christian Smith studied the religious beliefs of young adults in America. He coined the term "Moralistic Therapeutic Deism" to describe the lens through which many of them viewed God.[1] Smith claims that most young adults in America believe in God and even self-identify as Christian. However, when it comes to important questions of faith, he noted that very few people have solid convictions. Smith claims Moralistic Therapeutic Deism is the new religion of America's youth. Here are a few highlights of this particular religious paradigm.

1. God's chief concern is that people are nice and good. Good people go to heaven when they die (moralistic).
2. God wants me to feel good about myself and to find happiness on earth (therapeutic).
3. God doesn't want to be overinvolved in my life. But it is fine to reach out to God from time to time when I am really in a jam (deism).

I offer Smith's work as just one example of a less-than-useful religious map. There are of course others—for instance, the belief that God punishes sinful parents by striking their child with blindness. But in my experience most religious paradigms, ancient and modern, have one key ingredient: *they are fueled by an intense passion to get what we perceive to be fair.*

An Unfair God

The "Laborers in the Vineyard" (Matt. 20:1–16) is perhaps Jesus's most subversive parable. This parable has a timeless ability to tick us off. It's a story about a landowner who hires some day laborers to work his farm. Some began work at nine o'clock in the morning, some at noon, and some at three in the afternoon. Finally, a few others began work at five o'clock.

When the time came for the landowner to hand out paychecks, the five o'clock workers were paid the exact same as everyone else. This outraged the early morning workers because it violated what they perceived to be fair. To which the landowner, who represents God, responded: "Take what belongs to you and go; *I choose* to give to this last the same as I give to you" (Matt. 20:14, italics mine).

People struggled with the God map Jesus gave them in his teaching and parables. Jesus spoke of a God that wasn't fair, at least not as we understand fairness. Of course, the God Jesus spoke of was good, loving, merciful, compassionate, and kind. But for Jesus, fairness wasn't His Father's strong suit.

George Bernard Shaw once said, "God created man in His image and then man returned the favor." I believe that Shaw was right; we instinctively understand God through the lens of how we experience most people: as a *bookkeeper*. Our world keeps score, and so we reason that God must keep score, too. It may very well be that simple. We think it only fair that the first shall be first and the last shall be last.[2] We imagine that God's chief concern is that I am nice and that I live a good life and, assuming I keep my end of the bargain, that God owes me happiness in return. After all, *it would only be fair.*

We like bargaining with God. It's the reason our default religious instinct is to hand God a contract with incredibly childish terms. "Lord, I'll obey. I'll go to church. I'll read my Bible. I'll be a good person. And in return, I want you to bless me. Make sure nothing bad happens to me, that the market performs well, and let me die in my sleep when I'm ninety-three years old. And in the meantime give me X, Y, and Z because I need X, Y, and Z to be happy. Amen."

What typically follows is chaos. Perhaps we keep our end of the bargain, only to discover how painful it is that God refuses to play along. "How unfair," we think. Or maybe we come to terms with the fact that we're not as virtuous as we imagined ourselves to be, and when life turns sour we conclude that God is fair to punish us. We may even believe, as James Bryan Smith points out, that God is "eager to punish us for even minor infractions."[3] But in either case we are like people using a map of downtown New York to navigate the streets of Los Angeles. We can try harder, work on our behavior, or join another prayer group. But when it comes to seeing the Living God, we're still lost. Thankfully Jesus came to "seek and save the lost" and to give us a better map (Luke 19:10).

The Biblical Paradigm: One-Way Love

Eugene Peterson once said that the oldest religious mistake in the book is to assume that God has the same plans for us that we have for ourselves. I invite you to see Jesus's ministry as an attempt to remedy that mistake. God's plan for our life looks radically different than we think. The God map we've relied on may need to be torn to shreds.

Jesus offers us a completely new map. It's a map that reminds us that God doesn't love us in spite of our weakness, but rather that God loves us *in* our weakness. The purpose of Christianity is not to grow up spiritually so that we need God's mercy less. Rather, with Jesus we grow downward, we *descend*, to reach the end of our rope so that we might depend on nothing but the mercy of God. In Jesus we see that God loves struggling, broken people and that God delights in showering them with grace. Brennan Manning states:

> [God] is not moody or capricious; He knows no seasons of change. He has a single relentless stance toward us: He loves us. He is the only God man has ever heard of who loves sinners. False gods—the gods of human manufacturing—despise sinners, but the Father of Jesus loves all, *no matter what they do*.[4]

Grace is the love of God that emphatically proclaims that I am loved and worthy no matter what I do. It is precious, good, and empowering, but there is one thing grace is not: *fair*.

I understood grace for the first time in college. I visited Auschwitz, an internment camp in Poland where millions died during the Holocaust. Among those murdered was a Catholic priest named Maximilian Kolbe. It was at Auschwitz that I heard Kolbe's story for the first time. His final hour illustrates grace in a powerful way.[5]

In July of 1941 ten men in Kolbe's barracks were randomly chosen to starve to death. One man in particular cried out in fear. "I have a wife! I have children! Please, I beg you, take someone else!" When Kolbe heard this man's plea, he stepped forward, raised his hand, and spoke the following words: "I will die for that man."

Christians believe that this is what Jesus Christ has done for us. We have fairly been sentenced to die for our sins (Rom. 6:23). But Jesus Christ has died in our place. By the grace of God, Jesus has tasted death for everyone (Heb. 2:9). There is nothing fair about it.

Jesus's substitutionary sacrifice for us is God's grace made visible. The cross shows us a God that does for us what we cannot do for ourselves. No wages are due to us, and the cross reveals that we have not a single bargaining chip. As Thomas Merton puts it, God's love is so "infinitely good that it cannot be the object of human bargain."[6] To see God otherwise is to use a bad map. As Paul Zahl explains, "Grace uses no sticks and no carrots. It just dies for our life."[7]

Grace and Human Nature

Grace is the best news in the world. But for grace to offer true comfort, it must first offend our sensibilities. Indeed Jesus's message to our instinctual self is the worst news in the world. It announces that the first person singular we refer to as "I" has gone extinct. We can talk about Jesus being in the driver's seat all we want. But talk is cheap and Jesus invites us to relinquish our illusions of control. We're simply not competent to drive the car. Not even by a long shot.

Grace paints an incredibly flattering picture of God before it says anything good about us. God *chooses* to delight in us. God chooses to celebrate us, not because we are good but because God is. The bad news of grace is that my instinctual ego, which I wrongly label as my "self," is a spiritual corpse. The good news of grace is that Jesus raises the dead.

One of the things I am learning as a preacher is that people don't like being told that they're dead. We prefer the illusion that we are alive and free. Grace insists that *we are not*. Yes, we have a will, or a "chooser" as my friend Nathan likes to call it. We all make many decisions. Our decisions, at least without a certain degree of mindfulness, are so heavily influenced by our unconscious instincts and our social setting that it would be wrong to say that they are made freely.

For instance, suppose I put a whiskey in front of an alcoholic and he drinks it. It would certainly appear that he chose to take the drink. But would any of us say that in that particular moment he was free? Surely, he was not. And the same holds true for us.

I am aware that this is not the mental map most of us use to navigate life. We believe we are free to do what is right and that God fairly rewards those who make good choices. We may even see the Bible as God's textbook on how to choose good over evil.

But the Bible paints a much different picture of instinctual human nature. For instance, consider Abraham. Abraham was faithful, but was he good? This is the same man that gave his wife to a foreign king for sexual enjoyment on two separate occasions in order to protect himself. Then there's Elisha, a prophet whose self-esteem was crushed when some kids mocked him for being bald. Elisha's response was to pray, not for forgiveness, but that God would send a bear to come and eat them. Peter "the Rock" also fails to qualify as good. On the toughest night of Jesus's life, Peter took a power nap, chopped off someone's ear, and denied his Lord three consecutive times. What these examples illustrate is that God doesn't call us because we are good. God calls us because God is good, and for some reason unbeknownst to us, God thinks it a swell idea to shower us with love. This is the heart and soul of grace. We cannot describe ourselves as free any more than we can describe God as being fair. Paul Zahl describes grace like this:

> Grace is a love that has nothing to do with you, the beloved. It has everything and only to do with the lover. Grace is irrational in that it has nothing to do with weights and measures. It has nothing to do with my intrinsic qualities or so-called "gifts" (whatever they may be). It reflects a decision on the part of the giver, the one who loves, in relation to the receiver, the one who is loved, that negates any qualifications the receiver may personally hold.[8]

Atonement, Imputation, and Righteousness

Trying harder to be a better Christian is perhaps the most deflating thing we can do. It seduces us into thinking that a perfect moral record is the bargaining chip that God wants. But trying harder never works. I can try as hard as I want to dunk a basketball. I can put myself through rigorous training. But that won't change the fact that I am 5'6". Only if someone lifts me will dunking a basketball be possible. Otherwise, I will never be free to do a slam-dunk.

Jesus's sacrificial death on the cross for us is the elevation and freedom we need. Our deep shame weighs us down and keeps us from leaping. The impact of Jesus's death with us and for us is that all of humanity's shame is absorbed and dealt with. We have a new and unshakable status before God. Our current God map may or may not permit us to see that reality. But our inability to see that "there is therefore now no condemnation" does not make it any less true (Rom. 8:1).

If bargaining with God is part of our paradigm, we're lost and utterly out of touch with grace. We have the wrong map. There is nothing fair about God's love. Grace is not a two-way street. In Jesus, one-way love comes our way from God *just because*. Grace sees our failure and ugliness and imputes innocence and love to us. Grace woos our heart to believe and then takes our grace-fueled belief and accounts it as righteousness (Rom. 4:22).

The word *impute* means to ascribe qualities to a person that he or she doesn't naturally possess. Imputation takes a guilty person and calls him innocent. The impact of God's imputation, which is God's creative Word, is that as our eyes are opened we actually become as God regards us. We grow into the name that God gives us. We become lovely in the light of God's love. Such is the force of grace. We slowly become as God regards us. By nature our will is enslaved. Our chooser is broken. But grace breaks into our lives as a surprise and sets us free.

Imputation makes us present to a paradoxical reality. On the one hand we are sinful and guilty. We know this to be true. We daily experience the defects of our character. We daily are hurt by the defects of other peoples' characters. But on the other hand, God *declares* that we are good, innocent, alive, and righteous. God speaks the Word and calls good what by nature is broken and defective, but in doing so God simply reaffirms and recreates what is most true about us to begin with—our nature *is* perfection and sin is a disease that tears our divine nature apart. God's benediction makes alive what by nature is dead. The impact of God's Word is always that it *creates*. We become as God regards us, and we grow into the Word spoken over us. Not that we immediately experience ourselves as God regards us, nor do we always see in ourselves or others the new living being that God sees. We are, as Martin Luther noted, *simul iustus et peccator*—at the same time justified and sinful.

Confession shouldn't be an exercise where we name our sins and pledge to do better. Most people see confession as admitting their wrongs before God and promising it won't happen again. But it will happen again. And again. *And again.* Doing better is not something our chooser has the power to pull off. As Robert Capon notes, "Confession is not the first step on the road to recovery; it is the last step in the displaying of a corpse."[9]

And so a robust doctrine of grace does not have flattering things to say about humanity's instinctual nature when left to our own devices. Instead, grace announces overwhelmingly flattering things about human dignity. It says that we are the needy and blessed recipients of God's one-way love. Grace is a divine word that nourishes our spirit and deflates our ego.

The implication is that Jesus is not like a really good vitamin that we need to strengthen our ability and resolve to be faithful. Grace confesses that Jesus simply is Faithfulness Himself and reminds us that we are *in* Him. Jesus looks at each of us in love and announces, "I will die for that man. I will die for that woman." He has zero interest in improving the improvable. Jesus came to raise the dead by dying.

Growing in Grace: Learning to Accomplish Less

My friend Miles pastors a church that offers ten minutes of open space during their worship service. In open space, we listen to Jesus in our own creative way and make a personal response to the sermon. During one particular open space we were given a specific question to pray through: "What does God want me to accomplish in the coming year?" And in a rare moment of prayer I heard Jesus give a clear answer to my question. "Less," Jesus said. "I want you to accomplish less."[10]

Many of us see growth in the spiritual life as a process whereby we increase our capacity to do more for God. I would like to subvert that dominant paradigm and offer a better map in its place. *Growing in grace is about learning to accomplish less in the spiritual life.*

The truth is we simply cannot rid ourselves of the inner defects that enslave us. Throwing off the shackles of greed, ambition, lust, and jealousy is not a mere matter of willpower. We have no real capacity to change our own heart. Yes, we can practice mindfulness and learn to self-regulate, and we are responsible for doing so. After all, self-regulation is about holding our inner messiness in. But as we grow in grace, God cleans the inner mess *out*. This deep cleaning of the soul is simply not something that we can accomplish. Rather, we must learn to place ourselves in Jesus's presence so that the Spirit can do Her proper work.

Such is why growing in grace is a circular, lifelong process that involves three things. We grow in grace as we (1) see the cross, (2) accept acceptance, and (3) wait in weakness (see Figure 1.1). I believe that this simply *is* the Christian spiritual life. It is the non-work of transformation that God has given us to not do.

Figure 1.1

Seeing the Cross

In his letter to the Romans, Paul reminds us that "Christ died for the ungodly" (Rom. 5:6). Jesus's sacrificial death for us on the cross is the lifeblood of the Christian faith. It is what we are invited to see about God and about ourselves. God invites us to look *at* the cross as opposed to looking *past* it, as if the real point of our faith were found elsewhere. The cross *is* the point. We must heed Pilate's words and "Behold the man!" (John 19:5, ESV). The Spirit asks us to see God on the paradoxical throne we call the cross.

But we hate looking at the cross. We are fine speculating *about* the merits that flow from the cross. We are comfortable looking past the cross to some ideal we believe that Jesus's cross represents. But we simply hate looking *at* the cross because there is something about it that we don't want to see. The cross attacks not only the worst of human nature but also what we like to call the best of human nature. It reminds us that human selfishness worked *through* traditional religious observances and practices to put Jesus on the cross in the first place. The cross's message is that "we all like sheep have gone astray" and that we have zero power to rescue ourselves. We can only die with Jesus and wait in weakness for God to raise us.

But the story of the cross isn't the story we like to tell about ourselves. We prefer to see ourselves as seekers. We are people who can find our way to God if we try hard enough and engage in the right religious activities. Yes, we sin in the sense that somewhere along the line humanity took a wrong turn. But the cross is God's way of putting us back on the right road. Now it is up to *us*, we think, to exert proper effort and discipline so that we might walk in God's ways from here on out. It's all very flattering if you think about it.

But the cross tells a radically different story about humanity. It reminds us that we are hopelessly addicted to ourselves. We are the ungodly for whom Christ died. And it matters little whether we are addicted to what is profane or to what is noble. In both cases we are equally lost.

In the cross we have a road back home, for as we see the cross we relinquish the idea that we have any insight into what goodness or holiness looks like. Goodness and holiness, we believe, are found nowhere but the cross. Of course, to those of us who have been properly instructed in the ways of religion, the cross story will sound very foolish. But God's foolishness is more transformative than the collective wisdom of humanity (1 Cor. 1:25). It's a wisdom that reminds us that we don't just lack the willpower to be good; we also lack proper knowledge of what goodness truly is in the first place. We wouldn't know goodness—indeed we *didn't* know Goodness—when we saw Him. Otherwise, we wouldn't have demanded His crucifixion.

Thomas Merton reminds us that "God Himself was put to death on the cross because He did not measure up to man's conception of His holiness."[11] The implication of this, Merton says, is that if "we want to seek some way of being holy, we must first of all renounce our own way and our own wisdom."[12] The Christian must not see the goodness of Christ and dare try to imitate that goodness. She must *see the cross* and nothing else. Transformation happens only as God's Spirit draws us into the cross story so that the addicted "I" might be killed and then made alive again in Christ.

There is something within us that naturally despises what the cross actually says about our instinctual human condition. It exposes us as hopeless addicts with no internal resources to change. The ego experiences this news as horrible and tragic because we instinctively prefer some law or set of rules to follow that falls within our range of competency and skill. After all, obeying the law keeps us in control of our lives and makes us feel superior to others. Rather than relinquishing everything to God, following the law gives us a bargaining chip we think we can use with God. We tithe a portion of our self to God and continue doing what we instinctively want.

The cross is a haunting reminder that what we all instinctively want is *not God*. After all, humanity's instinct was to crucify the Son of God. The cross is not the foundation of the Christian religion. Rather the cross marks the end of religion once and for all and the beginning of something completely new. As Robert Capon states:

> Christianity is not a religion; it is the announcement of the end of religion. Religion consists of all the things (believing, behaving, worshipping, sacrificing) the human race has ever thought it had to do to get right with God. About those things, Christianity has only two comments to make. The first is that none of them ever had the least chance of doing the trick: the blood of bulls and goats can never take away sins (see the Epistle to the Hebrews) and no effort of ours to keep the law of God can ever succeed (see the Epistle to the Romans). The second is that everything religion tried (and failed) to do has been perfectly done, once and for all, by Jesus in his death and resurrection. For Christians, therefore, the entire religion shop has been closed, boarded up, and forgotten.[13]

The cross is only terrible news to that part of us that doesn't yet know that we have already died, a part that will fight like hell to save and justify ourselves. But to the spiritually awakened self within that knows it can accomplish nothing and that trusts God to do all the work, the cross is the best news in the world. After all, the cross doesn't only reveal our spiritual ineptitude. It emphatically declares that we are God's delight. In the cross we see that God has imputed righteousness to us just because He loves us; our new life in Christ is infinitely more real than the corpse we so frantically cling to.

It is not enough to merely see the cross. We must also embrace the grace that flows from the cross and accept acceptance. It is true that the cross marks the end of what we cling to as "our" life. But the cross is also the gate to a new life we already have, and indeed have always had from the beginning, which is hidden with Christ in God (Col. 3:3). We don't die in order to stay dead. We die in order to live.

Accepting Acceptance

As we learn to delight in our weakness, the cross becomes the best news in the world. In the cross we see that God has "lavished upon us" the "riches of his grace" and that God has "blessed us in Christ with every spiritual blessing."[14] We are fully and unconditionally accepted by God.

This is what salvation by grace is all about. The unconditional blessing of God is that we are accepted and loved because God chooses to accept us and love us. Accepting God's acceptance means that we let the love of Christ that surpasses all knowledge sink deep into the roots of our soul. We root our identity in the unconditional blessing of God.

In the Bible a blessing comes through the speaking of a word; *benediction* literally means "a good word." A blessing is a good word spoken about our true identity. A blessing carries creative power because we usually grow into what's been declared about us. For example, blame typically creates blameworthy behavior. Likewise, praise tends to create praiseworthy behavior. If someone tells us that we have a gift for compassion, we might find sparked within us a desire to become a more compassionate person. Blessings carry creative power. The word creates the reality, or "makes flesh."

We often forget how much words shape our life. "Sticks and stones can break my bones but words can never hurt me?" Counselors certainly know better. Negative words spoken over us years ago still operate as a present power. Even today negative words program how we "see" ourselves. "You'll never amount to anything." "You're disgusting." "You're just like your father." "You are so selfish." These words can do much more than hurt us. If spoken over us frequently enough, they can traumatize us and ruin our entire lives.

What's tricky is that the vast majority of the words that create who we become are much more subtle. The cover of *Cosmo* whispers, "Unless you look like this, you're not beautiful." The maledictions in this world are endless, and it's important we see how much is at stake. The words we internalize and allow to take root in our soul shape the person we become. Living words create us.

We root our lives in the grace of God only as we see ourselves as unconditionally blessed and accept acceptance. We hear the good word God sings over our lives and we joyfully embrace this divine benediction. We believe we are worthy of love and belonging because God says that we are worthy of love and belonging.

Believing this good news is at the heart of our human and spiritual development. We need someone that is valuable to tell us we are valuable. Someone that matters needs to tell us that we matter. Our desire to be blessed shapes our life, for good or for ill.

We see this principle perfectly illustrated in the story of the twin brothers, Jacob and Esau. Esau was the firstborn and his father's favorite. Jacob was a clean-shaven momma's boy. When Isaac was preparing to die, he wanted to give an official blessing to Esau. The common tradition at the time was to give one's wealth, power, and favor to the firstborn. Everyone else was ignored.

As a result, Isaac sends Esau out on a hunting trip. Isaac wants one last meal before he gives Esau his blessing. Meanwhile, Jacob is in cahoots with his mom because he wants to steal his father's blessing. This is the plan Jacob comes up with: he puts on Esau's clothes to look like Esau and puts goatskins on his hands to feel like Esau. Jacob lowers his voice to sound like Esau. Jacob steals a blessing by pretending to be someone he's not.

We are no different than Jacob. Our need for acceptance is so strong that we will do anything we need to do to feel accepted and blessed. This is because the world we live in doesn't issue unconditional blessings. This is a problem because we all have a deep and divine need to feel accepted and blessed. Our world says that to be blessed we need to perform, look good, stay young, and be funny, clever, interesting, or rich. The world's blessing is only awarded to people that earn it. The world doesn't just dole out acceptance for free, and the *default instinct of the human heart is to project this anti-grace nonsense onto God.*

We imagine that we need to pray more or bring more people to Christ or make a bigger splash in the world before God will accept us. Or perhaps we tell ourselves that God has no resources but us; if we don't step up to the plate and come through for God, then the whole gospel project will fail. We fear that there is something we must do to find divine acceptance. We forget that grace doesn't use sticks and carrots, and that it expects nothing from us at all. Grace just dies for our life. As Thomas Merton explains,

> The beginning of the fight against hatred . . . is not the commandment to love. . . . It is a prior commandment, *to believe.* The root of Christian love is not the will to love, but *the faith that*

one is loved. The faith that one is loved *by God.* The faith that one is loved by God although unworthy—or, rather, irrespective of one's worth![15]

Brennan Manning tells a great story of what accepting acceptance looks like in practice. An Irish priest stumbles upon a peasant praying by the side of the road. The priest is impressed and says to the peasant, "You must be really close to God." The peasant's response reveals a deep understanding of God's grace: "I am," he said, "because God is so very fond of me."

Paul Tillich once said that faith is the courage to accept acceptance. We instinctively want to do something and prove that we are worthy of acceptance. We want to feel like we are a superior person and that we deserve what we have. But we're not. And we don't. And that's why accepting acceptance is an incredibly courageous act. It is perhaps the most countercultural thing we can do. Seeing the cross, we accept acceptance and relinquish our instinctual belief that God requires something more than faith in God's goodness. This truth humbles us. It makes us feel our deep vulnerability and teaches us to wait before God in weakness.

Waiting in Weakness

I recently came down with a nasty sickness. I fall ill every year between Thanksgiving and Christmas. Typically there is nothing I hate worse than being sick. But this year, in an odd moment of grace, I found myself thanking God for my sickness. A part of me was genuinely grateful for the debilitating experience of being sick. I realized that sickness always makes me do what worship, Bible study, and prayer are supposed to make me do: wait before God in weakness. This posture of expectant waiting is indeed the proper end of all spiritual practice. We increase our capacity to wait before God in weakness where we plead for God's mercy, beg for God's grace, and ask God to make us whole.

Thomas Merton said, "There is no greater disaster in the spiritual life than to be immersed in unreality."[16] The reality of the human condition is that we are sick and that our case is terminal. Our life may be a *slow process* of loss and decay. But life simply is a process of loss and decay nonetheless. Jonathan Edwards said that the story of Job is the story of us all. Job lost his family, health, wealth, and status all in one day.[17] We may experience our losses more slowly, but eventually we all end up at death's door being asked to relinquish everything to God in trust.

My favorite biblical example is John the Baptist a week or so before he dies. Before his imprisonment, John was a firebrand that shook people into a state of readiness for Jesus's arrival. "Prepare the way of the Lord," he shouted, "make his paths straight" (Matt. 3:3). John is confident, secure, and energetic. There is no doubt, uncertainty, or hesitancy in his voice. But weeks later John finds himself in prison where he awaits execution. Suffice it to say this is not how John thought things would end. John is deeply confused, and so he sends whatever friends he's got left to see Jesus with a question: "Are you the one who is to come, or shall we look for another?" (Matt. 11:3).

John's question arises from a deep place of vulnerability. John has lost his ministry, his following, his freedom, and his influence. He is now on the verge of losing all hope. John is close to despair and he can't help but wonder if Jesus is truly Israel's long-awaited Messiah. John finds himself at death's door being asked to relinquish everything to God in trust.

If we go through life without ever experiencing such a moment, I'd question how honest we are being with God and with ourselves. In the end, we all lose everything we fight so hard to protect. Our youthfulness disappears. No diet or surgery can stop aging. We have a child, get married, get divorced, change jobs, or move to a different city—with all that change comes loss. And then of course there is catastrophic loss. This is the loss that brings us to our knees and makes us ask the exact same question as John the Baptist. *Jesus, where are you? I'm in prison here! Aren't you the Messiah? Should I be waiting for someone else?*

As we grow in grace, we find in John a spiritual companion. We see a man that is confused, questioning, and weak, but yet who still clings to Jesus in faith. This is a reflection of ourselves. We humbly acknowledge our loss, limits, and the reality of our weakness. From that place we wait in trust for the surprising gift of God's resurrecting grace.

As Christians we acknowledge that we live in a very confusing in-between time, the "already, but not yet" time. Christ's death and resurrection are behind us. Our salvation and resurrection are already accomplished on the one hand. But on the other hand, the cosmic unveiling of that eternal truth has not yet been revealed. We live in weakness, and we wait to discover ourselves already raised in splendor and strength.

Growing in grace is not about becoming spiritually strong and ridding ourselves of weakness so that we feel the weight of Jesus's cross less. Rather, as we grow in grace we embrace our weakness so that we see Jesus's cross more personally. In the words of Thomas Merton:

> If we know how great is the love of Jesus for us we will never be afraid to go to him in all our poverty, all our weakness, all our spiritual wretchedness and infirmity. Indeed, when we understand the true nature of his love for us, we will prefer to come to him poor and helpless. We will never be ashamed of our distress. Distress is to our advantage when we have nothing to seek but mercy. We can be glad of our helplessness when we really believe that His power is made perfect in our infirmity.[18]

Paul once tried to explain this principle to the church at Corinth. The Corinthians were being influenced by slick preachers that offered them a recipe for growing strong in the faith. Paul reminded them that grace was counterintuitive. Grace says that God's power is made perfect *in* our weakness—not in spite of our weakness. "Therefore I will boast all the more gladly of my weaknesses," he said. "For when I am weak, then I am strong" (see 2 Cor. 12:9–10, NIV).

Christ has already raised each one of us in strength. We have a new resurrected life hidden with Christ in God (Col. 3:3). At the end of time, the trumpet will sound and we will experience our resurrected self fully. But in the meantime we wait in weakness. We even thank God for our brokenness. Our frailty helps us see the cross more clearly and empowers us to accept the acceptance that flows from it. For whenever we are weak, *that* is when we are strong.

Dying to Live

Henri Nouwen tells the story of a Lutheran bishop imprisoned in a German concentration camp. An S.S. officer tortures him in the hope of forcing a confession. But the bishop had a remarkable tolerance for pain and didn't respond to the torture. This enraged the abuser so much that he beat the bishop harder and harder until finally the officer broke down in frustrated exhaustion. "Don't you know that I can kill you?" he screamed. The bishop looked his torturer in the eyes and said very slowly. "Yes, I know—do what you want—but I have already died."[19]

This story is a reminder that Jesus Christ didn't die to make me spiritually strong. He died to raise me from the dead and to set me free. I believe freedom grows only as we acknowledge that the grasping, egotistical life that we so violently cling to was already drowned in the waters of baptism. We have a new resurrection life hidden with Christ in God. The Christian life isn't so much a climb as it is a fall into grace. Christian spirituality, or a life of prayer, is about descending into God, and into our own soul, to discover this divine life hidden in our depths. This is so difficult and contrary to instinct because currently my dead life is the only life I see. And that's the reason it is a life I must relinquish, for my dead, egotistical life is what keeps me spiritually blind.

The good news is that Jesus doesn't have a problem with people that are blind. It's the control freaks too stubborn to admit that they actually need glasses that Jesus has a hard time working with. The first thing grace teaches us is to admit that we are blind, for to confess that truth always means that we see a lot more than we think.

Discussion Questions

1. How does this chapter challenge your "God map"? What did you find to be most confusing about this chapter? Most hopeful?

2. Do you believe that God is "fair"? Why or why not?

3. This chapter asserts that grace assumes a low view of human nature and a high view of human dignity. Do you agree? What is the difference between the two?

4. In what sense can accepting God's unconditional acceptance be a countercultural act? In what areas of life do you find it most difficult to "accept acceptance"?

5. "God's strength is made perfect in weakness." Do you agree? Is there a time in your life when God's strength was displayed in and through your weakness?

6. What does the phrase "see the cross" mean to you? How is seeing the cross different from theorizing *about* the cross? Where do you see the cross most frequently in your life?

7. Do you believe that people are born spiritually blind? Why or why not?

CHAPTER

2

Relinquishment

"The alternate choice to becoming more than we are is trying to hold on to the life we have." —*David Benner*

"God creates everything out of nothing—and everything which God will use he first reduces to nothing." —*Søren Kierkegaard*

"Christ says 'Give me All. I have not come to torment your natural self, but to kill it.'" —*C. S. Lewis*

like control. My instinct is always to play it safe, and I have no natural appetite for risk. I remind myself of Ben Stiller's character, Reuben Feffer, in the romantic comedy *Along Came Polly*. In this particular movie Stiller plays a risk analyst with such a strong need for prediction and control that he uses a computer program to make all of his choices. Feffer's life strategy is simple: always stay in control and take the least risky path.

Our instinct for control and risk aversion runs deep. I realized this last week when I sat down to prepare a teaching on the biblical story of Pentecost. I was stuck and having a really hard time crafting my message. So after four hours of staring at a blinking cursor, I snapped: "I hate Pentecost!"

That's when I realized that I had found my message, or perhaps that my message had found me. The topic of my sermon was about how much I hated Pentecost.

I don't mean I hate *the idea* of Pentecost. The story itself as recorded in the Acts of the Apostles could not be more inspiring. I love that God sent the Holy Spirit to infuse the life of the Church, which is what Pentecost is all about. As a theological truth, Pentecost is lovely and quite comforting. I just instinctually hate what Pentecost says about my life. Pentecost reminds me that I am not in control of my own destiny.

A Journey of Descent

Words shape what we have the capacity to see. The language we use to describe the spiritual life matters tremendously. The spiritual life is often described as a journey of ascent. We talk about growing *up* spiritually, and living our lives *above* reproach. Benedict even urged his monks to *ascend* the ladder of humility. We think the way to God is up.

The language of spiritual ascent is not unbiblical, nor is it altogether harmful. But ascent language can, and often does, reinforce a false mental map that leaves us in control of our religious destiny. As a result, we assume that God wants us to muster our willpower and strive with all we have to grow up into the person God created us to be. We want to heed Paul's charge to "take hold" of abundant life (1 Tim. 6:19). What we all too easily forget is that to take hold of a new life we must first relinquish our old one. The point of the spiritual life is not to take control, but rather to relinquish all that we are and all that we have to God in faith. In the words of Thomas Merton, "In order to live I have to die."[1]

It is far more useful and hopeful to speak of the spiritual life as a journey of *descent*. We grow up by growing down. We become spiritually taller as we become smaller. In this descent mental map of the Christian faith, we find power through weakness, life in death, and freedom as we relinquish control.

We may wonder why God prefers to work this way. I don't have a good answer to that question. But I believe that given the limitations of human nature, relinquishment is the only way to God. We don't like to admit this, but the default, instinctual formation we all receive sets us up to fail; we quite simply do not have the resources to make it on our own. Before we have the capacity to think, we have already been programmed to crash and burn.

Consider a helpless infant. He doesn't have language to communicate, but he does have instinctual needs. The second we leave the womb, our bodies cry out for security and affection. Shortly thereafter, we manifest a deep, instinctual need for power and control. We jokingly call this the "terrible twos." The toddler feels an ingrained need to get her own way. When our instinctual need for power and control is thwarted, we throw tantrums. All of this happens at the level of instinct long before we can reason.

What's fascinating about the human brain is that every experience we've ever had is stored in our nervous system like a file on a computer. Most experiences our conscious mind has forgotten, but nothing has been erased. Indeed every experience we've ever had is "stored" in our body. This is perhaps most true of experiences that carry the strongest emotional charge—moments when our grasping for security, affection, power, or control were either satisfyingly met or painfully denied us. They are moments that were particularly frustrating or gratifying, and although the memories of these moments have been forgotten or repressed by the conscious mind, the emotional charges associated with these experiences remain stored in our body and "ready" to manifest themselves. And it takes very little to trigger these old emotions and the instinctual reactivity that goes with them.

The impact of these unconscious memories is that a gap exists between what we think drives us and what actually does drive our lives. We are all at least somewhat driven by instinct, which is to say that we all have some autopilot set of behaviors that we rely on to get our unconscious drives for security, affection, power, and control met.[2] Thomas Keating calls them our "emotional programs for happiness," and he notes that the primary spiritual challenge is to identify our unique programming so as to ensure that our default, unconscious instincts don't keep us from a deep encounter with God.

This then becomes our greatest spiritual challenge: God created us to flourish as we extend self-sacrificial love to one another, while we have been programmed to grasp, claw, and compete to ensure that our wants and needs are met. Like lower forms of life, instinct drives the vast majority of what we do and how we experience our world. We may rationalize our instincts with well-polished narratives about why our autopilot preferences and habits are right and those of our neighbors wrong. But for the Bible to make any sense at all we need to wrestle with its claim that not one of us instinctually seeks to honor and glorify God through a life of self-sacrificial love. It is not our instinct to find our life by losing it.

The essence of the spiritual life is the relinquishment of all that we are and all that we have to God. Our deepest instincts are not useful when it comes to a deep encounter with Jesus. This is especially true if our chief instinct is to gain power and control over others. Keating notes that "such persons are programmed for human misery. In trying to control situations and other people, they are in competition with five and a half billion other people, many trying to do the same impossible thing."[3]

I attended a conference last year on family therapy and counseling. The keynote speaker did not speak from a Christian perspective, yet he offered tremendous insight into the instinctual side of the human being. In particular, he noted three questions that drive our life as we navigate our respective relationships.[4] These questions live deep beneath the surface of our conscious mind. They exist at the level of instinct.

What do you think of me?

Do you accept me?

What do you want me to do?

I was keenly aware during this lecture that by the time most of us arrive at adulthood, we are both driven by and shaped by these three questions. At a certain stage in life we make choices about what we need to do or who we need to be for others to accept us and think well of us. *This is precisely what it means for us to take control of our life.* We make choices to tame the chaos, and the choices we make work their way into our instinctual programming. Put differently, at first we make our own choices, but at some point it's the accrued choices we've made that start *making* us.

We may not feel like we are in control, but our instinct is always to take control nonetheless. Unfortunately, our control instinct doesn't die the moment we begin an intentional relationship with Jesus. In fact, many of us actually experience our need for control amping up in the early stages of our spiritual development. Our need for control may even be what makes following Jesus seem so attractive. Perhaps we assume that Jesus wants to help us take control of our messy lives. And so we read the Bible, go to church, and shape up. We want God to think well of us. We want God to accept us. We yearn to know what God wants us to do. We think Jesus offers a moral path, a religious high road, and a way for us to take control of our life. All the while we stay blind to Jesus's chief message that he came to *take* the very life we are so desperate to control and to save.

Nothing inside of us instinctually wants to see the cross, accept acceptance, and wait in weakness for God to work in and through us. That would mean admitting that we are not in control. We prefer improvement, which allows us to stay in control. But no one wants to experience death, the falling out of the only life we know, that always precedes resurrection. Resurrection means we first have to die, to fall, and to relinquish the only life that we know.

A Different Way of Being Christian

A group of college students recently asked me to come speak to them about why I was a Christian. I quickly realized that we were working with two different ideas about what the word *Christian* meant. So I subversively redefined the word Christian for them. I wanted to ensure that we were working with the same mental map.

Many people hear the word Christian and immediately think of someone like Hilary Faye from the movie *Saved*. There's a scene in *Saved* where Pastor Skip enlists Hilary Faye to intervene in the life of Mary. People fear that Mary is backsliding, and so Pastor Skip tells Hilary to be a warrior for Jesus and to bring Mary back into the fold. He reminds Hilary that only someone who's spiritually armed can guide Mary back to faith.

Hilary Faye interprets Pastor Skip's words in a curious way. She attempts to kidnap Mary and perform an exorcism. Hilary screams at Mary, "We need to get rid of the evil in you! Jesus loves you!" Mary understandably freaks out, doing all that she can to break free. After barely escaping Hilary's surprise exorcism, Mary tells Hilary Faye that she doesn't understand the first thing about love. Hilary's response is classic. She pegs Mary in the back of the head with her massive Bible, and then screams at the top of her lungs: "I am filled with Christ's love!"

Hilary Faye is obviously a caricature of what many people imagine when they think of a Christian. But I also think that many Christians can identify with the character of Hilary Faye perhaps a bit more than we care to admit. We think of ourselves as warriors for Jesus. We see our assignment as getting rid of the evil *out there*. We think that God wants us to seize the initiative and to stay spiritually armed.

The Christian that embraces Jesus's way of descent looks much different. As we grow down spiritually, we relinquish more and more of our life to Jesus. Like Abram, we hear God's call to leave what we know and can control; we risk venturing with God to a land that we do not know and that cannot be tamed. We confess that our instinct to preserve our life will be the very thing that kills us, and we admit that, if left to our own instinctual devices, we will most certainly crash and burn. We choose the way of descent and ask Jesus to teach us to die in order to live.

How I Learned Not to Trust God

At the heart of the spiritual journey lies a choice: *In whom will we put our trust?* (Ps. 25:1–3). As we walk Jesus's way of descent, we come to see only two possible choices. We can put our confidence in ourselves, or we can put our confidence in Jesus Christ.

One of the hardest things for a Christian to see about him or herself is his or her utter lack of confidence in Jesus. If you are unsure of how little (or much) you actually trust God, pray for revelation, and when God's revelation crushes you, enjoy a fall into grace. See the cross, accept acceptance, and wait in weakness for God to create more trust in your heart.

There should be nothing shaming about admitting that we do not trust God. In fact, telling the truth about our lack of confidence in Jesus is the doorway to liberation and faith. Our autopilot instinct is not to trust God, but rather ourselves, and in most areas of our lives our faith simply is not in Jesus. Yes, we want Jesus arguing our case postmortem before God. We believe he died to erase our sins. Our mind clings to the doctrines of our faith. But only a small part of our heart is fully relinquished to Jesus's purposes. It's our emotional programs for happiness that are actually driving the car.

The reason there should be no shame in our admission that we lack confidence in Jesus is that life teaches all of us how *not* to trust God. For instance, my parents divorced when I was in the fifth grade. This was a season in life when I felt especially depressed. I remember sitting on a psychiatrist's couch feeling lost and hopeless. As tears streamed down my cheeks, I asked the therapist where God was in my pain. He didn't know, and I certainly hadn't a clue as to God's whereabouts. The impact of this experience is that I believed *in* God, but my heart felt *abandoned by God*. The Bible assured me that God was with me, but my heart, and my instincts, told me just the opposite.

It would be wrong to assume that I'm just talking about people with unhappy childhoods or that only the severely wounded have a difficult time with trust. I had a wonderfully happy childhood and I am blessed with wonderful parents. I experienced so much more joy than I did pain. I simply offer one illustration of how I learned *not* to trust God.

Sadly, there is nothing about growing into adulthood that magically erases all the painful experiences that are stored in our body, filed away in the deep places of our heart. Perhaps we have grown up, but few of us have grown *past* these experiences. We haven't processed the wounds and integrated their lessons into our soul. Therefore, yesterday's wounds are easily reactivated today. And so while every day I wake up, shave, put on a suit, and pretend like I'm an adult, at the deep emotional level of instinct, it's the same "me" crying on a therapist's sofa. It takes very little to trigger my experience of feeling abandoned by God. And when my abandonment button gets pushed, my heart is *not* relinquished to God. It's relinquished to my instinctual, emotional programming.

Of course, many object: "That's all in the past!" We say this because we do not see our past as the primary driving force that shapes our present experience. This is a mental map I find to be most useful:

> The past, until Christ does His healing work, is the primary force
> that drives our present experience. Healing will only happen in areas
> of our life that are relinquished to God.

I invite you to consider what it would mean for your life if this were true. How might this particular mental map of the Christian faith change areas of your life where you've been stuck for years, or improve your most significant relationships? Ponder where you might need to relinquish control and what past wounds Jesus might want to heal.

It is *this map* that has changed the way I experience God and think of myself. It's a map that enables me to tell the truth about how I learned not to trust God. I responded to my deep feeling of abandonment by making a decision: "I will do whatever it takes to keep people from leaving me." I took control and answered the human heart's three instinctual questions for myself.

1. I will make sure you think well of me.
2. I'll say or do anything to get your acceptance.
3. What do you want me to do? I will do *anything* to keep you from leaving.

Of course, I made this decision subconsciously, slowly, and over time. Many experiences, wounds, and unmet needs went into it. It was still *my* decision though, a spiritual transaction that I initiated about who I needed to be in this world to survive and find acceptance. It was a decision that left me as I wanted: fully in control of my life. And as I increasingly made that decision, that decision *increasingly made me*.

My experience as a pastor is that most people, spiritually and emotionally speaking, are in the exact same place. It doesn't matter how polished our resumé or how well we present ourselves. It's still a presentation nonetheless. And I believe this to be true for all people. Our parents, professors, priest, president, and plumber are just like us on the inside. We all have the same fears and wounds. We just make different decisions about what we need to do or not do and who we need to become as a way of coping with our fears and wounds.

Confidence in Jesus Christ is hard. The way of descent is not primarily about trusting in our ideas about Jesus or perhaps in some heavenly arrangement that He's made on our behalf. It is about relinquishing all that we are to Jesus and putting our confidence in Him *now*. This will necessarily mean unmasking the many ways we are programmed to place our confidence in ourselves. As David Benner notes, the essence of faith is to "trust that we are being led to a place that we do not know, on a journey that we do not control."[5] There is absolutely nothing about what Jesus offers us that we instinctually prefer.

The Fruit of Relinquishment

In the Kingdom of God, we die in order to live. We relinquish the small life we do know in exchange for a much fuller and more meaningful life that, at present, we lack the capacity to see. But the end game *is* life. We die so that we might be raised. "Unless a grain of wheat falls into the earth and dies," Jesus said, "it remains just a single grain; but if it dies, it bears much fruit" (John 12:24).

It's important to acknowledge that the resurrected life we receive back is not a life we can imagine or predict. We do not relinquish our ego to receive back a much larger warrior-ego for Jesus. While it is a life marked by greater faith, we do not experience our newfound faith as robust certainty but as an increased need to cling to Jesus and each other in the midst of all of our uncertainty. We experience a greater level of brokenness than ever before. It's not that we *become* more broken. On the contrary, as we relinquish our life to Jesus we fall into a grace-full life that's much more whole than the life we formerly knew. It's just that we experience ourselves as more broken because Jesus is ripping away the illusions we have relied on for so long to shield us from the experience of our brokenness. In the process, we become less defensive. Indeed a less defensive and more vulnerable life posture is the primary fruit of relinquishment. We find freedom in knowing that there is nothing in us worth defending in the first place, nor is there anything that needs to be defended. Our life's work is to see the cross, accept acceptance, and wait in weakness for God to act. We haven't the time for anything else.

Increasingly we come to experience faith as *unknowing* as we learn the art of relinquishment. Formerly, our religious ego was strengthened in what it knew about God, but now, the more we attach to Jesus, the less we attach to our ideas about Jesus. We come to see that godliness without contentment isn't godliness at all (1 Tim. 6). For the essence of godliness *is* being content with whatever God has seen fit to give *us*. We don't need more than what God has provided. We trust that God knows what is best, and that the little light we do have is more than enough to sustain us in our journey. We are no longer in control.

This experience teaches us to wait in weakness. We see how silly it was to bargain with God in the first place. God is free to give. God is free to take away. We come to understand what it means to truly receive something from the hand of God.

This might not be what you signed up for when you dropped your net to follow Jesus, but it simply *is* the fruit of relinquishment: a greater experience of brokenness, faith as unknowing, and an increased capacity to wait in weakness.[6] This simply *is* the life Jesus offers. Relinquishment is the spiritual non-foundation upon which all of Jesus's work in and through us is built. We may not like it, but in the Kingdom of God we die in order to live.

Baby Steps

At this point, you may be present to a fairly serious problem. Our inner self's furniture needs to be thrown out, or if nothing else it needs to be radically rearranged. We understand that we have *some* part to play in this process of spiritual relinquishment. And yet, it is the "I that needs to die" that refuses to let go. Our addicted self, which is hell-bent on preserving itself, needs to die, and yet it is our addicted self alone that can relinquish itself to Jesus. Eugene Peterson explains our spiritual quagmire quite well:

> The capacity to make a decision, to direct life, to exercise freedom is the very thing that needs developing if I am to make a decision for Christ. . . . Without an exercised will, I am a dishrag, limp in a dirty sink. . . . But the moment I begin exercising my will, I find that I have put a fox in charge of the chicken coop.[7]

There is no easy way out of this dilemma. Only our will can freely relinquish itself to God, and yet it is our stubborn will that is the problem in the first place. We are the chief resistor against what God longs to do in our life, and yet it is also we who invite Christ into our life. I offer no tidy solution to this problem, but an image from one of my favorite movies comes to mind.

In *What About Bob?*, Bill Murray plays the character of Bob Wiley. Bob is an incredibly earnest and sincere man who suffers from multiple phobias. He makes an appointment to see New York psychiatrist, Dr. Leo Marvin. Dr. Marvin has a massive ego and prescribes his own book entitled *Baby Steps*. He tells Bob not to focus on the big picture, but rather to set small reasonable goals. "Take life one day at a time," he says, shuffling Bob out of his office. It's an incredibly silly movie, but when it comes to relinquishing our life to Christ, I find the advice to be spiritually sound. We take baby steps.

We cultivate whatever inner stillness, solitude, and mindfulness we can manage today. We make one courageous choice to slow down the pace of our life. We take a deep breath and remind our anxious heart to accept the acceptance that is already ours. We remind ourselves there is nothing we can add to Jesus's finished work. We intentionally engage at least one difficult person in our life. We lift our hearts to the Lord and ask, "God what are you trying to do in my life in and through this person?" We choose love. And when we find ourselves overcome by failure and shame, we see the cross, accept acceptance, and trust that God's strength is made perfect *in* our weakness. After a year or so of baby steps, we find that we have decreased and Christ has increased (John 3:30). We are not sure how it happened or when it happened, but our hearts are more relinquished to Jesus Christ than they were before. Baby steps over the span of a lifetime add up.

Life in the Middle Voice

I know that baby steps won't fully resolve our little theological dilemma. Our problem is that God must initiate, guide, and sustain *our* work—which we both want and don't want simultaneously—of relinquishing all that we are to Jesus.

Our mental map of how God's will intersects with our ability to choose relinquishment should be as clear as possible as we embrace Jesus's way of descent and allow ourselves to fall into grace. Unfortunately, our language doesn't allow for much nuance. Our thoughts easily get stuck in binary "this is all God's work" or "this is all our work" categories. Relinquishing ourselves to Jesus Christ is both God's work and ours. The spiritual life knows *nothing* of either/ or thinking.

Eugene Peterson says that the spiritual life is lived in the middle voice. The middle voice is a particular nuance of Greek grammar.[8] In the *active* voice we initiate an action that impacts someone else: "I counsel my friend." In the *passive* voice we receive the action that someone else initiates: "I am counseled by my friend." But in the *middle* voice, we are active participants in the results of an action that someone else initiates: "I take counsel from my friend." My friend initiates the counsel, but still *I* must be willing to take it.

We who embrace Jesus's way of descent live in the middle voice. We do not initiate anything worthwhile, but rather respond to the Spirit and take baby steps to cultivate stillness, space, solitude, silence, and openness. We look for words and actions already initiated by our Savior. We then take counsel from Jesus our friend. We actively participate in what God has willed and already set into motion. We don't seek to manipulate God with our bargaining, nor does God manipulate us. But as Peterson says, "We learn to live with praying—willing involvement in an action that we do not originate."[9]

It is much easier to give up control when we see that we were never in control of our life in the first place. The truth is we never give up control. What we actually shed is the *illusion* of being in control. We can't give up something we never had in the first place, and the vast majority of life cannot actually be controlled. Most of life is entering into what is already there, and what is "already there" is stronger than we are. Our genetics, family, and the many social systems we are a part of shape us much more than we shape them. These are not things we chose for ourselves, but rather aspects of our life that first chose us.

Few of us appreciate the role passivity plays in our lives. Marriage is the perfect example. In the early stages, the two lovebirds stick together like Velcro®, and their two wills fuse into an undifferentiated state of emotional bliss. But real life eventually happens. Life gets more complicated. Obligations, necessities, routines, and demands begin to crowd in on us, and when this happens, what it means to love changes drastically. Love ceases to be an ecstatic feeling of euphoria and becomes a dance we must learn. This is where passivity and what's "already there" come into play. Just try dancing without paying attention to the tune, the dance floor, and where the feet of your lover want to go; it doesn't work. The dance gets frustrating, awkward, and painful really quickly. That's why we either learn to enter the dance or else we storm off in search of a new dance partner. This is what I mean by passivity. *The dance is already there.* Our job is to first learn the moves, and only then can we begin thinking about what a new and better dance might look like.

Our relationship with God is like a dance. We don't lead, but we're also not dragged around the dance floor against our will. We follow God's lead. It is not purely passive, but passivity still plays a key role. This is life in the middle voice.

Willingness or Willfulness

We who embrace Jesus's way of descent really only have one spiritual task. We must cultivate willingness to follow God's lead.

Willingness is not the same as willfulness. Willfulness is about the assertion of our ego. It is our readied posture to lead the dance and to control our environment. Willfulness is about the full expression of our ego that does not want to die and that instinctively chooses anything that can protect it from death and resurrection. Our will always chooses the small life it does know over the new life it doesn't know. It refuses to risk relinquishing itself to the purposes of Jesus Christ. Willfulness is what shields us from a deep encounter with God. It is *willingness* that we must cultivate.

Robert Capon offers an image that helps me distinguish between a middle-voice willing life and an active-voice willful life. He writes the following:

> I want you to hold out your right hand, palm up, and imagine that someone is placing, one after another, all sorts of good gifts in it. Make the good things whatever you like—M&M's, weekends in Acapulco, winning the lottery, falling in love, having perfect children, being wise, talented, good-looking, and humble besides—anything. But now consider. There are two ways your hand can respond to those goods. It can respond to them as a live hand and try to clutch, to hold onto the single good that is in it at any given moment—thus closing itself to all other possible goods, or it can respond as a dead hand—in which case it will simply lie there perpetually open to all the goods in the comings and goings of their dance.[10]

Jesus's way of descent doesn't mean we turn our nose up at the dance of being alive. It just means we cease clutching to our dance partners—our family, friends, coworkers, and anyone else with whom we have to deal. We stop needing them to dance a certain way for us to feel okay. We ask God to take the lead. We respond to life as a dead hand. This is what relinquishment to Jesus Christ is all about. It's about learning to live by first learning to die.

The School of Gethsemane

Jesus stands ready to teach us His art of prayerful descent, which He does by first pointing us to His own life. Jesus's life was a continual relinquishing descent to the cross. "Though he was in the form of God, [Jesus] did not count equality with God a thing to be grasped, but emptied himself, by taking the form of a servant" (Phil. 2:6–7, ESV). Richard Foster calls this "the school of Gethsemane."[11] He reminds us that the night before Jesus died, he wanted a way out. Jesus begged His Father to let the cup pass and Jesus suffered under the weight of His Father's silence. Jesus willingly relinquished his will to the Father: "Not my will but yours be done."

Foster says, "We do well to meditate often on this unparalleled expression of relinquishment."[12] In Gethsemane, we see the Son of God begging his father through blood-soaked tears and having his request denied. This is the essence of relinquishment. It's a life where God closes more doors than God opens so that we might experience God's loving presence in that place of no escape.

There is nothing more contrary to instinct than relinquishing our life to God. Life is wrought with so much pain. Our instinct is to run away from the pain, but relinquishment lowers us into its depths.

Our instinct is always to take control and fix the situation. Maybe it is a shaky marriage, a sick child, or a complicated work situation. Maybe we need this person to shape up or that person to function differently. Perhaps we're nearing retirement, and we realize that we're not prepared. Relinquishing these and the many more fears that haunt us can seem an impossible task.

Perhaps you now understand why I instinctively hate Pentecost. My mind knows that relinquishment brings with it a priceless treasure, but my heart has a hard time letting go. But let go we must in order to taste the freedom that God created us to enjoy. We do not die to stay dead. *We die in order to live.* As Richard Foster writes,

> Crucifixion always has resurrection tied to it. God is not destroying the will but transforming it so that over a process of time and experience we can freely will what God wills. In the crucifixion of the will we are enabled to let go of our tightfisted hold on life.[13]

A relinquished, palms-open life is far from easy, but at the end of the day it's the only real life there is. If our clutching ego is running the show, it's not living, just surviving. Jesus invites us to something infinitely more rich and significant than mere survival. "I came that they may have life, and have it abundantly" (John 10:10).

Let go. Live your life with palms wide open. Take baby steps towards a more willing life. In the Kingdom of God relinquishment is not *a* way to life. It is *the* way. Plus, it's all got to die eventually anyway. Let it die now. Jesus is so much better at resurrection than you are. Pentecost isn't that bad, after all. It's actually quite healing. I promise.

Discussion Questions

1. Do you believe that the essence of the spiritual life is the relinquishment of all that we are and all that we have to God? What does the word "relinquishment" mean to you?

2. What aspect of your life do you most try to control? What aspects of your life are most relinquished to God?

3. Do you think that the "deep instinctual side" of our humanity is useful in the spiritual life? Why or why not?

4. What painful experiences have you had in life that make trusting God difficult?

5. Do you think the spiritual life is an "ascent" to God or a "descent" to God? Can both be true? What are the strengths and limitations of each metaphor?

6. Do you think that the fruit of faith is a greater experience of brokenness? Why or why not? Does true faith lead to a greater knowing or "unknowing" of God?

7. What is the difference between willfulness and willingness? Which of the two is more useful in the life of faith?

3

Healing

"Prayer heals the emotional wounds of a lifetime." —*Thomas Keating*

"Looking to the past illumines the present. But make no mistake about it; it is painful." —*Peter Scazzero*

"I am the Lord who heals you." —*Exodus 15:26*

There's an old tale about a scorpion and a frog. One day the scorpion decides that he needs to cross a river. Since scorpions can't swim, he asks a nearby frog to carry him across the river. The frog was hesitant. "I know how dangerous you are," he said. "If I let you get on my back, you will certainly sting me and I will die." "That's ludicrous," the scorpion replied. "Think about it. If I sting you, we will both drown."

The frog needed more assurance. "How can I be certain you won't just wait until we are safely on the other side of the river before stinging me to death?" "I would never do such a thing!" said the scorpion.

"How could I? I would be far too grateful for your help to sting you." The frog pondered the scorpion's words and reasoned that this scorpion wouldn't hurt him. "How could he?" the frog thought, as he let the scorpion onto his back.

The frog began to swim across the river, gradually feeling safer and safer. But about halfway across the river, the scorpion stung the frog. "You fool!" croaked the frog in agony. "Now we will both drown! Why did you sting me?" The scorpion replied as honestly as he could: "Because I am a scorpion. It is in my nature to sting."

This tale captures our experience as human beings. We want to live lives of mutuality and cooperation, but far too often our instinctual programming sabotages our deepest desires. We resonate deeply with Paul's experience: "I do not understand my own actions. For I do not do what I want, but I do the very thing I hate" (Rom. 7:15).

The Experience of Wounding

The changed life many Christians claim to experience doesn't go to the roots of their soul, but remains cosmetic in nature. We learn to hide our stinger behind religious clothing, or perhaps we build a spiritual life around being ashamed of our stinger. Sadly, few of us get to the deep, painful work of letting Jesus heal our inner scorpion.

The Bible portrays Jesus as a man deeply interested in healing people. Jesus healed the blind, the lame, the deaf, and the demon-possessed. He also healed people's inner shame and the instinctual fear that drove their life. Jesus's healing went to the roots of people's soul. Jesus even compared himself to a physician. "Those who are well," he said, "have no need of a physician, but those who are sick" (Mark 2:17). Jesus didn't come to call the righteous, but rather people who needed healing in the deep places of their soul.

Jesus's way of descent is not about leaving our self *behind*. Jesus does not ask us to abandon the self that we know, but rather to relinquish it to God. Indeed it is not our deepest self that needs to die, but rather our stinger—the grasping ego that instinctively wants to control its own fate—that needs to die. Our deepest self, created in the image of God, needs healing and restoration.

As we descend into the arms of Jesus we find that God's love begins to heal the wounds of a lifetime. We find our unique stinger softened and less poised for action than it was before. As David Benner notes, our descent into the loving arms of Christ "cannot help but engage these broken parts of us and bring healing to the fragmentation and inauthenticity that has resulted."[1]

Many of us are unaware of just how badly life has wounded us. Of course, some of us are hyperaware of our wounds, and some of us even build a life around the pain we have experienced. If this is the case, our identity is found in a story we tell where we're the victim and someone else the perpetrator. Or perhaps we've built a life around *not seeing* our wounds. Our defense mechanisms are impenetrable, so much so that not even we can get through to ourselves.

Jesus invites us to see our wounds more objectively. He asks that we relinquish our wounds to Him in exchange for healing and a fresh purpose. Our world classifies people as either a victim or a perpetrator. But Jesus doesn't see some of us as frogs and others of us as scorpions. We are all implicated in the world's wounding cycle of violence. The world stings all of us and, because getting stung repeatedly hurts, we adopt an unconscious, instinctual way of being to avoid getting wounded again.

Brené Brown uses the metaphor of armor to speak about our unconscious, instinctual way of protecting ourselves from pain. She says we put on vulnerability armor that shields us from getting hurt. But not only does the armor we wear keep us from authentically connecting with others, our armor is usually what stings other people. Our armor is a response to the armor of other people, and it's our armor that creates the armor of other people. Put differently, my stinger doesn't protect me from your stinger. It creates your stinger.

This is what Jesus Christ invites us to see. All are victims. All are perpetuators. There are no exceptions. Brown writes:

> As children we found ways to protect ourselves from vulnerability, from being hurt, diminished, and disappointed. We put on armor; we used our thoughts, emotions, and behaviors as weapons; and we learned how to make ourselves scarce, even to disappear. Now as adults we realize that to live with courage, purpose, and connection— to be the person whom we long to be—we must again be vulnerable. We must take off the armor, put down the weapons, show up, and let ourselves be seen.[2]

Jesus longs to bring healing to the deep places of our lives. He wants to go to the roots of our soul and clean out the gunk that keeps us perpetually stinging one another and running away from the stingers of other people. His way of descent has nothing to do with putting on spiritual armor, but about relinquishing control so that God might heal our depths and strip us of our instinctual need to wear armor in the first place.[3]

Recall the Bible's narration of humanity's tragic fall from grace: Adam heard footsteps, felt fear, saw his nakedness, experienced shame, seized control, and chose to cover himself with loincloths—his very own armor, so to speak. Healing begins the moment we see this pattern in our own life. We confess the unique way that we feel fear, cover ourselves in protective armor, and do what we must to divert attention away from our spiritual nakedness.

And the wounds we've suffered are not always big or even obvious. In fact, most of the wounds that create the armor we wear aren't obvious at all.

For instance, we get picked last at recess. Or we get glasses and people laugh. Maybe our older sister has always outshined us and no one ever celebrates us. We get verbally, physically, or sexually abused. We fail a class, don't get the job, or get a divorce. Someone speaks a really careless word that calls our whole identity into question. These and the countless other wounds we experience in life are ways we hear the world telling us that we are not worthy and loveable. As a result, we wrongly conclude that if we want to be worthy and loveable, we better "armor up" and get busy being a different person.

As a pastor, I find myself curious by the stories people tell me when they are scared, frustrated, depressed, or angry. I've noticed that no one ever tells me the story of what actually happened to him or her—"the facts" so to speak. Instead they tell me the story of what it meant to them. They tell me who is to blame. They tell me about the decisions they've made to shield themselves from future heartbreak. The story they tell me always has them playing the role of the helpless victim, and then they tell me how they've responded to make sure he or she will not be a helpless victim ever again.

People rarely tell their story of heartbreak objectively. Our default isn't to say, "I called a girl, asked her out, and she said no." The story we tell is, "I called a girl, asked her out, and she rejected me." These are two very different stories. We invested the second story with a particular meaning: "I am not enough." She rejected me.

That's our main problem. We get wounded and then we tell some story to ourselves and to other people, if only subconsciously, about how what our experience of wounding really means is that something is wrong with us and that we are not enough. The problem with our version of the story, aside from it being untrue, is that we're then forced to armor up—that is to make choices about how to deal with our perception of not being enough.

Perhaps we choose to be cool. "I'm just not interested in dating," we say. Or maybe our response is to work really hard and excel in school. "Who has time to date?" we think. Maybe we choose to become a jerk. "Women are idiots," we say. Maybe we choose to numb the pain: ice cream, booze, a weekend marathon of *Breaking Bad*. Or, we tell ourselves she said no because [fill in the blank]: "She said no because I don't drink, because I'm too skinny, or because of the way I dress." So we start drinking, working out, or wearing trendier clothes.

This is how our false self, which is conceived in the lies we believe about our experience of wounding, begins to form. Again, the facts in this particular illustration are quite simple: "She said no." That's it. But that's not the story that any of us instinctively tell. The story we tell ourselves about this experience is always some form of "I am not enough," and as a result we adopt a whole host of unconscious and instinctual behaviors that we think will either make us feel like we're good enough or, if nothing else, that will shield us from future pain.

The Source of Wounding

When we experience great pain, our instinct is always to ask why. We want an explanation, or if nothing else we want someone to blame. We feel a need to rationalize what happened and tell some story that makes sense to us. But learning to simply see our wounds more objectively and to hold them before God in faith is the major task of the spiritual life. We cannot descend with Jesus into wholeness if we're clinging to lies about "why" life hurts so much.

The cause of our suffering is always far more complex than whatever story our mind cooks up. The truth is there is never any one person or group of people we can blame for our pain. A fearful mind that is not relinquished to Jesus Christ will always tell us that the opposite is true. A mind whose autopilot instinct is to ask and answer the "why" question is really skilled at finding someone to blame. When this happens we come to hate our ex-spouse, the person that ran over our dog, or the pharmaceutical company that won't save my life by selling me their drug at a reduced rate. An anxious, controlling mind always finds someone to blame and answers the question "why" in such a way that it makes us the victim and someone else the perpetrator. However, the truth Jesus invites us to see is that we are all both victims and perpetrators in the world's wounding cycle of violence. Everyone is always and everywhere *both*, and there are no exceptions to this rule.

The source of our wounds is not easily traced. Our wounds stem from intermingling sources that we can never untangle. Some wounds come from our own blind, foolish, and sinful behaviors. Other wounds come from the hurtful and selfish behaviors of others. We suffer other wounds because we sometimes experience our world as imperfect and cruel. Tsunamis take out entire cities. Plagues and illness spread through villages. Babies are born with serious genetic defects. As Glen Scorgie puts it:

> The wounds we acquire in the course of simply living our lives have many forms. It is painful just to think about them. They include traumatic memories, living with a disability, genetic disorders, mental illness, the dark cloud of depression, psychological fragility, damaged emotions, diseases, chronic pain, life regrets, confused sexual identity, and an uncertain sense of self—to name just a few. The scope of all the pain is staggering. There are so many ways in which we are not well.[4]

This is what Jesus invites us to see as we take off our armor: namely, that every last one of us is *unwell* and is in need of deep soul healing. In fact, apart from this assertion, the basic tenets of Christianity and the promises of Jesus are incoherent. Seeing the cross, accepting acceptance, and waiting in weakness only make sense as a life strategy for people that need healing. Not only does Jesus want us to see that we are all *unwell;* he also wants us to see that we are *all* unwell. Otherwise we will fail to see the manner in which compassion and a deep empathy for others is at the heart of the Christian life. As we descend with Jesus into wholeness, we become known for our deep compassion, both for ourselves and for other people. There will be more about this in chapter six.

The Bible tells us that when Jesus saw the crowds, "he had compassion for them, because they were harassed and helpless, like sheep without a shepherd" (Matt. 9:36). The Greek word translated compassion (*splagchnizomai*) conveys deep emotion. A literal translation of the Greek text is that Jesus was moved deep in his bowels. Jesus wants to reprogram our instincts so that we're moved by compassion for others from deep within ourselves, too.

Descending to wholeness will lead to a more compassionate life, but this necessarily means seeing all of our wounds more objectively. Practically speaking, we cannot take up our cross if we're stuck blaming someone for giving us that cross. God asks us to take up our cross and to die daily. This simply *is* the Christian faith.

Jesus is moved by compassion for us all. We may not yet feel this reality to be true at the level of our instinctual programming, and so patience is needed because deep healing takes time. As we relinquish the lies that drive our life, we find that compassion wells up like a fresh spring from within, washing off the crusty lenses that far too long have left us blind and staggering.

Self-Knowledge

As we experience healing we receive a new map through which to navigate life. Healing and self-knowledge are deeply intertwined and they cannot be separated. Imagine self-knowledge as your right leg and healing as your left leg. Let's say we take a step with our right leg by growing in self-knowledge. We will not be able to take a second step with our right leg until our left leg catches up. Our healing will be stunted if we do not grow in self-knowledge. In the same way, the healing we experience will be limited if we refuse to grow in self-knowledge by seeing what subconscious instinctual forces are really driving our life.

The vast majority of what drives human behavior lies beneath the surface of our conscious thought. Consider the example of an iceberg: only about ten percent of an iceberg can be seen by the human eye. Taking control of our spiritual lives doesn't work because the tip of our iceberg is all that *we* have access to. But the instinctual programs for happiness driving our behavior live in the deep waters beneath our consciousness.

Our life is just like an iceberg. There is so much more that we do not see than we do see. Beneath the iceberg of our lives are things we don't know about ourselves. These are the areas of unconscious incompetence that perpetuate the cycle of wounding in our life.

Most Christians engage a spirituality that is cosmetic in nature, a spirituality that is limited to the tip of the iceberg behaviors. We learn to spend more time in prayer or we work on being a kinder person. Of course, these are all very healthy and even necessary spiritual practices, but that doesn't mean they're practices that force us to relinquish ourselves to Jesus Christ. Surface practices cannot deal with the wounding that lives in the deep waters beneath our consciousness. Only Jesus has access to those waters. Diving into these waters is what our fall into grace is all about. We throw ourselves into the deep waters of our faith, allow ourselves to sink, and we experience Jesus's soul-healing that comes with a deeper knowledge of both God and our self.

Many Christians know that Jesus invites us to know God at a deeper level, but few understand that Jesus also invites us to know *ourselves* at a much deeper level. In fact, the invitation to know God and to know ourselves cannot really be separated. We can know wonderful facts about God and never get to know ourselves. But memorizing dogma rarely creates a greater level of self-awareness, and sometimes the inner rigidity that makes us cling to dogma is the very thing that prevents us from growing in self-knowledge. But as we encounter the Living God, we also encounter the "living" us—the "us" that swims below the surface of our conscious mind and that which is cradled in the arms of Jesus.

An anonymous philosopher put it like this: "The recipe for perpetual ignorance is to be satisfied with your opinions and content with your knowledge." Or as the author of Proverbs (4:7) sarcastically says: "The beginning of wisdom is this: Get wisdom." What both thinkers imply is that we are not instinctively wise when it comes to knowing ourselves, and that when it comes to the Christian life, what you don't know *will* hurt you, and other people as well.

Many people assume that Jesus didn't have to work at growing in self-knowledge because he was God. But Jesus was also fully human. The Bible says Jesus "had to be made like his brothers in every respect" (Heb. 2:17, ESV). We can't assume that Jesus bypassed the process of discernment whereby he accepted his vocation to be Israel's Messiah and the Savior of the world. Indeed the Bible portrays Jesus as a man that was very eager to grow in self-knowledge and God knowledge. As a child, Jesus listened intently to the religious scholars and asked questions (Luke 2:46). He routinely awoke before his disciples to spend time in prayer (Mark 1:35). He also asked his disciples: ". . . who do *you* say that I am?" (Luke 9:20).

The pursuit of self-awareness was a big part of Jesus's ministry. As Jesus grew in experiential knowledge of His Father, He was strengthened in the knowledge of His true identity as God's beloved Son. The same holds true for us: as we grow in the experiential knowledge of God, we come to know ourselves at a deeper level.

Jesus invites us to learn why we instinctively respond in predicable ways to certain situations, why the same bad habits and attitudes trip us up time and time again, as well as why this person makes us so angry or that future scenario makes us so scared. At present, we don't know what we don't know about ourselves. Like the man by the pool of Siloam, we were born blind (John 9:7). According to family therapist Michael Kerr, a screen of subjectivity exists between our world and us. "The screen appears to get thicker," he writes, "as we get closer to observing ourselves. The closer we get to ourselves, the greater the pressure to see what we want to see or, at least, to see what we have always seen."[5]

It is precisely this subjective screen that Jesus removes as He heals us, for it is our experience of wounding that keeps our screen intact. Healing and self-awareness are inextricably bound together. As we seek healing, we pray as blind beggars: "Lord, let me recover my sight" (Luke 18:41, ESV). Then we act on our prayer by submitting to two core disciplines that are indispensable to the healing process: the prayer of *examen* and the experience of a grace-full community. Only as we practice these two disciplines do the scales fall from our eyes so that we may know ourselves more fully, even as we have been fully known by God all along.

The Prayer of Examen

The first spiritual discipline essential to the healing process is the prayer of *examen*, which is a phrase I borrow from Richard Foster. Two biblical truths shed light on the value of the prayer of examen's role in our spiritual life. The first truth is that the Spirit of God lives inside of us (1 Cor. 3:16). The second biblical truth is that "the Spirit searches everything" (1 Cor. 2:10).

God's Spirit lives inside of us and is always searching—not only to see what's beneath our iceberg, but also to see whether or not our conscious mind *wants to see* what God sees. The prayer of examen happens when we intentionally open our hearts to the Lord and desire to see what the Spirit of God longs to reveal. We ask God's Spirit to search us and to reveal to us what's actually inside of us. We want to see the instinctual programs driving our behavior. We want to see the anger, pride, lust, and fear. We want to see the wounds we have experienced and the armor we have put on to make sure we do not experience wounding again. The prayer of examen happens as we desire to see what creates pain in our life and in the lives of the people we love. We admit that we were born blind and we pray that God might open our eyes. It is a contemplative practice through and through—a waiting in weakness for the Spirit to show me *myself*.

We practice the prayer of examen to open up to the Spirit of God so our mind can reflect on how God has been present to us throughout the day. God is always speaking to us, though we rarely hear God's voice in the moment. We must develop the habit of divine listening and grow in our desire to prayerfully review our day through spiritual eyes. Richard Foster says, "We prayerfully reflect on the thoughts, feelings, and actions of our days to see how God has been at work among us and how we responded."[6] We look at what happened to us and how we felt about it. We look at our instinctual response. We note painful patterns that keep repeating themselves. We pay special attention to emotions that were particularly high or low. We wonder before the Lord: What is behind my disappointment? My cynicism? My need for this person to like me? My recurring fantasy that has me telling that person off? Why did this person's compliment mean so much to me? Why am I always so quiet around that person? We pray with the psalmist: "O Lord, you have searched me and known me!" (Ps. 139:1). We then ask for a revelation: *Spirit of God, you search and know every aspect of my soul. Please tell me what you see!*

I recently had an especially fruitful time of examen. I felt very discouraged because a particular relationship I was involved in wasn't bearing fruit. Specifically, I mentored a young man named Hector in the juvenile prison system for nine months. I valued our time together and thought Hector did as well. Upon his release, we both wanted to continue our relationship in the outside world. So we met at McDonalds a few times to grab a burger, chat, and play cards. But after a few weeks, Hector quit returning my texts. He is now locked up in a different prison where I can't see him.

The emotions my conscious mind could acknowledge were disappointment and bewilderment. This is what I brought to God in our time of examen. I felt disappointed in Hector for flaking out on me, and perhaps a bit angry at God for letting him do so. I brought these emotions before the Lord in a posture of curiosity and openness. God showed me some difficult things about my character on this particular day.

I heard God telling me that I expected Hector to fit into my busy and controlled life. Hector sensed that he was a slot on my calendar, not a priority. I expected Hector to work around my schedule, and I had zero intention of working around his. I was not really available to Hector.

God also showed me my fear: I would never tell Hector where I lived, nor would I invite him into my home. God reminded me that we are created in the image of the Trinity, and that we are hardwired to connect to others with a deep and primal need to belong to a community. God told me that if the Body of Christ would not welcome Hector into their home, it was natural for him to return to his gang. God showed me how my fear had a part in creating Hector's life.

God also showed me how I entered into my relationship with Hector expecting something specific in return. I expected Hector to get better. I also expected to feel better about my life of privilege for spending time with someone less fortunate than myself. God gently reminded me that unconditional love is offered with zero expectations.

Of course, it wasn't totally negative. God was proud of me for being open to the truth. God was pleased that I was willing to see the truth because it meant I felt secure in God's one-way love that is always offered without condition or expectation.

All of that self-knowledge was the fruit of opening my heart to the Spirit. I just laid my disappointment before the Lord in a posture of curiosity and openness and listened. That's what the prayer of examen is all about. We acknowledge that God is present in the concrete details of our life as a Friend, Lover, Teacher, and Spouse. We ask God to open our eyes to the Presence we're typically oblivious to. We listen in openness and truth. We see the cross, accept acceptance, and wait in weakness for a fresh word from the Lord. We want to learn about what lies beneath our iceberg. We thank God for searching our heart and showing us what's there. We don't lose ourselves in self-flagellating apology, but we also refuse to fall back on the litany of self-justifying defense mechanisms we've relied on for years that keep us from seeing the truth. We just open our heart to the Spirit and *see*. That's it. We're content when there is no revelation. We thank God for any revelation given to us. We don't fix whatever God shows us. That isn't our job. Our job is to tell the truth about the broken places inside of us that need healing. This is part of what it means to wait in weakness before the Lord.

It is important that we not lose sight of the big picture. The prayer of examen is a means to an end. The goal is to grow in self-knowledge so that we might relinquish ourselves more fully to the will of God. Paul urges us to offer all that we are as a living sacrifice to God (Rom. 12:1). This offering by which we relinquish our full self to God is not some abstract theological principle. It is perhaps the most practical thing Paul says, and to make such an offering we must first see our broken self and resist whatever temptation there is to reject what we see or to fix what we see or to try to create something different than what we see. Instead we simply *offer what we see to God* as a living sacrifice. Relinquishment means coming to terms with the concrete details of our life. Relinquishment means accepting whatever it is that makes us tick and befriending the instinctual programming that governs our behavior. Richard Foster offers:

Who we are—not who we want to be—is the only offering we have to give. We give God therefore not just our strengths but also our weaknesses, not just our giftedness but also our brokenness. Our duplicity, our lust, our narcissism, our sloth—all are laid on the altar of sacrifice.[7]

The goal of the spiritual life is not to rise above our nature, but rather to lovingly descend through it. Healing happens as we grow in knowledge of our unique self's nature so that we might accept it and relinquish it to God for God's purposes. Put differently: *We can't relinquish something to God that we can't see.* This is precisely why the prayer of examen is indispensable to the healing process.

However, individual examen is not enough. To grow in self-knowledge and find healing we must also experience a grace-full community that is committed to telling us the truth.

Grace-Full Community

We know how hard it can be to find our way into an intimate and grace-full community. We also know the reason why true community is so hard: *other people.* I say that partly in jest, but of course it's always true that people are difficult. *We* are difficult. As Henry Nouwen once noted, "Community is that place where the person you least want to live with always lives."[8]

Community may be hard, but we hunger to experience intimate relationships with other people. We long to belong to a grace-full community where we are fully known and accepted. God wired us for genuine and meaningful connection with other people, and yet we find that we're sometimes allergic to the very relationships that our hearts so desperately long for.

Our failure to form healing relationships with others is in large part due to our brokenness. Larry Crabb reminds us, "Brokenness is a condition, one that is always there, inside, beneath the surface, carefully hidden for as long as we can keep a façade in place. We live in brokenness."[9] He suggests that spiritual community is so rare because we're ashamed of our brokenness. "We'd much rather be impressively intact than broken. But only broken people share spiritual community."[10]

I believe that only a grace-full community heals human brokenness. Crabb reminds us that healing is not a "repair job on what is wrong inside of me that will lessen my struggles."[11] Healing has nothing to do with experiencing fewer struggles. It's about finding the freedom to relinquish our full selves to God in the midst of our struggles in the firm and certain knowledge that God will redeem those struggles and use them for our good. Healing happens as we learn to celebrate this truth of God's redemptive power together in community.

This necessarily means finding other Christians who share our longing to relinquish every ounce of our life to God. It also means relinquishing our instinctual quest to hide. We put our anger, fear, powerlessness, desires, and mistakes on display. We give our stinger a name. We tell others the truth about what's inside of us that they don't see. We listen in gratitude as others tell us what's inside of us that *we* don't see. And somehow, in a way that can't be explained but only experienced, when two or three come together in Jesus's name by giving up their quest to hide, the Spirit moves. People are healed. I've seen it happen and I've experienced it personally.

But not just any community will do. Grace, which is the one-way love of God that is always offered without condition or expectation, must be the foundation of the community. Grace must also form the walls, floors, ceiling, and roof. In practice, nothing said or heard in the context of a grace-full community should scandalize or shock us. We assume the fragility and brokenness of human nature. There is nothing inside of you that is not also inside of me. Acceptance, worth, and value are not up for grabs in a grace-full community. The Christian Gospel assumes that we are all more broken than the façade we wear *and* that we are much more loved than we have the capacity to fathom. Unconditional acceptance is the foundation of a grace-full community. The faithfulness of Jesus Christ holds the true spiritual community together. We flat out assume that *we* are not faithful. Only broken people that know they need healing experience spiritual community.

The impact of being part of a grace-full community is that transparency flows. *We tell the truth.* There is no self-knowledge without truth, and there is no healing without self-knowledge. We tell the truth about what we see in ourselves. We tell the truth about what we see in others. We speak the truth in love. My willingness to be vulnerable creates in you a desire to be vulnerable, too. There's something about this experience of non-condemning truth telling that heals us.

A grace-full community is healing for two key reasons. First, it asks us to disclose our brokenness to other people. Self-disclosure is always wounding when grace is not the foundation of a community. That's the reason we've learned to hide in the first place. Our default setting is to be ashamed of our brokenness. As a result we criticize, judge, fix, withdraw, lie, and offer unwanted advice. But a grace-full community that gathers in the name of Jesus is different. We tell the truth about our brokenness only to find that a ring is put on our finger and that a party is being thrown in our honor. And *that* experience of grace and unconditional welcome heals us every time.

The second reason grace-full community is healing is because it reveals our blind spots. We recall that the subjective screen between our world and us gets thicker and crustier the closer we get to observing ourselves. As the old saying goes, "The eye cannot see the eye." But your eye *can* most certainly see my eye, and my eye can see yours. That means I've got the key to your self-knowledge. And you've got the key to mine.

The prayer of examen will only take us to the edge of the cliff in our quest for self-knowledge. We need a grace-full community if we're serious about jumping. Consider King David. David was so immersed in unreality, so blinded by his lust for power (and Bathsheba) that he was blind to what everyone else around him could see. David was only a great King because he had a Nathan in his life—someone that loved him enough to tell him the truth (see 2 Sam. 12:7).

We all need a handful of Nathans in our life—people we can trust with the fullness of our story. Without a Nathan there is no healing. We need people that love us enough to tell us the truth about what they see in us. I don't mean people that readily spray their anger onto us and tell us off. Nothing is more wounding than the experience of another's rage. I mean people that know their own brokenness and hunger for healing themselves and who know in their bones that our healing is intertwined because we are all members of One Body.

One of my "Nathans" is a friend named Patrick, whom I have coffee with every Monday. Patrick cares about me and often begins a sentence by saying, "John, you might not know this about yourself, *but.* . . ." Now that is a spiritual friend. Patrick and I comprise a very small grace-full community. That's why I commit myself to the friend-ship. It is healing. My life is more relinquished to God because of my friendship with Patrick. I have grown in self-knowledge because of our many conversations, and I now see more of myself that I can relinquish to God.

Experiencing Grace, Discovering Purpose

The knowledge of God's grace doesn't heal lives. The *experience* of grace heals lives. This is precisely what happens in a grace-full community. Not only do we find healing in community, we're also reminded that God heals us for a purpose. The Christian belongs to the world. We are taken and blessed only to be broken and sent out.

We can discover our purpose only as we experience grace and find healing in the deep places of our lives. Earlier we used the metaphor that likened healing and self-knowledge to two legs. Take a step with one leg, and the other leg needs to catch up.

The same analogy holds true for healing and purpose. As God heals us, we live into our purpose. As we live into our purpose, we find fresh healing. Henry Nouwen says we become "wounded healers" as we experience grace in community. "Changing the human heart and changing human society are not separate tasks, but are as interconnected as the two beams of the cross."[12]

God does indeed soften our stinger. That's what healing is all about. But like Jacob, we leave our encounters with God limping. We're present to more joy and pain than before we encountered God. We discover that we are both healed and more broken all at the same time, and that the two experiences are one in the same. We find strength as we fall deeper into a grace-filled life of waiting and weakness. And in the midst of our waiting we come alive with fresh purpose.

God heals our stinger and leaves a massive scar in its place. Our unique purpose in life is no doubt mysterious, but one thing I know for certain: *it has everything to do with what flows out of that scar.*

Discussion Questions

1. Do you believe that you need spiritual "healing"? If so, from what? Where in your life have you experienced healing before?

2. Do you think that we have a tendency to play the victim when we are in pain? Why or why not?

3. Do you think that all people are *both* victims and perpetrators? Is there such a thing as a "pure victim"? Why or why not?

4. What does it mean to live a "compassionate life"? How does one grow in compassion?

5. Can the knowledge of God and the knowledge of self be separated? Can you grow in one and not grow in the other?

6. Does the experience of healing lead to fewer struggles? Why or why not?

7. What is your experience of grace-full community? What does it mean for you to extend grace to another person?

CHAPTER

4

Purpose

"Do not pray for tasks equal to your powers. Pray for powers equal to your tasks! Then the doing of your work shall be no miracle. But you shall be a miracle." —*Phillips Brooks*

"They were saints in that most effective and telling way: sanctified by leading ordinary lives in a completely supernatural manner." —*Thomas Merton*

"One thing is necessary. Mary has chosen the good portion, which will not be taken away from her." —*Luke 10:42 (ESV)*

recently attended a rehearsal dinner for a dear friend's wedding and was seated next to a young married couple whom I had never met before. The wife's name was Anne, and the husband went by Nate. Anne was clearly pregnant and so, after making appropriate small talk, we asked Anne about her baby. Anne beamed with joy as she relayed the news that she was expecting a baby girl, and as the conversation progressed Anne talked about her pregnancy with all the normalcy and excitement that one would expect from an expecting mother.

The first conversational pause came when someone asked Anne a question about her little girl's future. Maybe the question had to do with the quality of public schools in her city, or perhaps the question had to do with whether or not Anne was planning to quit her job to become a stay-at-home mom. This was the first time I ever felt a pause.

"My baby is sick," Anne said. She paused again briefly, and then went on to explain that her little girl Ava had an incredibly rare disease. There was a fifty percent chance that the baby would die during labor, and no one really expected Ava to live past the first few months. Anne then told us that ninety percent of women in her situation terminate the pregnancy.

Anne gripped her husband's hand and softly explained that she and Nate felt called to bring Ava into the world. In all the pain, sadness, and brokenness, Anne and Nate were present to a divine purpose: they wanted to give birth to baby Ava. They believed that by doing so, God would bring healing and wholeness to others.

I remember being struck by Anne's rare blend of vulnerability and confidence. Anne wasn't deluded or in denial. Quite the opposite was true. Anne and Nate thought through their decision prayerfully and carefully. They wept together daily, and they told the truth about both the darkness and the light that filled their lives as they pondered what it would mean to bring baby Ava into the world.

Anne also told us that she felt a deeper joy, solidarity, and compassion than she had ever known before. This experience was breaking Anne open, and hope, healing, and courage flowed from Anne's soul to whosoever had the courage to listen to her story. My brief encounter with Anne changed me. As she wrote in her blog, "Ava was not a random happening, but instead a little gift who was entrusted to us for a specific purpose."[1]

The main impact of my encounter with Anne is that it makes me think about my own divine purpose. I think about Anne and wonder what God wants to give birth to in and through my life. Indeed, I don't think it's possible to follow Jesus and not wrestle with that question. Our spiritual fall into grace may be a life of relinquishment, but relinquishment is not the same thing as disengagement. As we descend with Jesus into a healed life, we find ourselves engaging the world more wholeheartedly.[2] We find ourselves wanting to give birth to something unique, so that our story of wounding might bring healing and wholeness to others.

A Life of Engagement

God does not shower us with grace and heal our wounds to give our ego the safety, comfort, and control that it craves. God heals us so that we might live into our purpose. Indeed, our healing is stunted and remains incomplete until we find and enter into our divine purpose. There is something specific that God wants to bring into being in and through each one of our lives. No two people are the same. We each have a unique set of gifts, wounds, life experiences, circumstances, and temperament, and as a result God wants to give birth to something unique in and through our very different lives. My purpose, therefore, is the unique way that the Kingdom of God can only grow and expand through me.

Until we experience some measure of healing, we never live into our purpose simply because we continue to live from a false self. There is no divine purpose without integrity—that is without becoming wholly ourselves. Our purpose is to become our true self; and as we become our true self, we live into our purpose. As Thomas Merton explains, "Humility consists in being precisely the person you actually are before God, and since no two people are alike, if you have the humility to be yourself you will not be like anyone else in the whole universe."[3] Our divine purpose is not to become more like somebody else, but rather to discover and grow into our true self. Such is why there is no purpose without healing, and likewise there is no experience of healing that does not put us in touch with our unique purpose.

As we experience healing and discover our true self, we begin engaging the world from a place of vulnerability and openness—not as a perfect self, but as a cracked, imperfect, and yet far more confident self. Our true self is not a perfect self, but rather a lighter, kinder, more aware self that is enlivened by the grace of God.

No one else can tell you what your divine purpose is. It is better to err on the side of saying too little about our divine purpose than to risk trying to say too much about it. If you have not discovered it for yourself, it is not uniquely your own.

Our divine purpose is also something that we must constantly *rediscover*. The paradox of our divine purpose is that it always remains the same, and yet at the same time it is always changing. What never changes is the shared purpose Christians have to engage the world in a way that bears witness to Jesus's love. What does change, and exponentially at that, is the world that we are called to engage, as well as the person that does the engaging.

Our unique purpose is elusive and something of a mystery. It is not something we understand by looking directly at it. Rather, we first peel away the layers of misunderstanding that shield us from seeing what our purpose truly is. We begin by describing what our purpose is not, and only then can we begin to say anything coherent about what our divine purpose actually is. Only then does our purpose begin to show itself to us. After all, we do not find our purpose; our purpose always finds us.

There are two layers of misunderstanding that need instant peeling away if we are to discover our purpose. These obstacles keep us from seeing the unique way that we might engage the world in a way that brings healing to others. The first is our fear of being ordinary, and the second obstacle is our anger.

The Fear of Being Ordinary

Our fear of being ordinary keeps us from living into our purpose. We so badly want to be extraordinary. We're always looking for a bigger stage, or to make a bigger impact. Living the life we actually have with integrity and character doesn't feel very significant. We wonder how we can live into our purpose when we're swamped with emails, dirty diapers, and spend half our week in a cubicle. "Certainly people who've found their divine purpose do more than *this*," we think. But whatever *we* are doing never feels like quite enough.

When we're scared of being ordinary, nothing ever feels like it's enough. We don't feel special enough, seen enough, or heard enough. We don't have enough people to support our cause, or enough money to fund it. We don't have enough energy to do more than we're already doing, or enough talent to do it if we wanted. Or so goes our scarcity-riddled reasoning when we're plagued by a fear of being ordinary.

The cultural consensus is that an ordinary life is a worthless and meaningless life. Most people would rather be called anything other than ordinary. But the truth that God would have us hear is that all people, from an eternal perspective, are both incredibly ordinary and eternally unique all at the same time. That is why our divine purpose has less to do with what we do than it does with the sort of person we become in the midst of our unique and quite ordinary lives.

But unlearning the cultural verdict that an ordinary life is a meaningless life takes time and prayer. It involves seeing that God delights in using ordinary people to accomplish extraordinary, albeit secret and often hidden, things. The scandal of the incarnation is that the Son of God took on flesh in and through a quite ordinary Palestinian Jew.

God entered the world in a secret, hidden, and ordinary way, and hardly anyone at the time noticed. God did not choose a home in Athens or Rome, nor was Jesus born in some extraordinary palace. Quite the contrary, the Son of God was born in a cave in a forgotten corner of the Roman Empire. The birth of Jesus was so incredibly ordinary, and that's precisely what makes it so extraordinary in the eyes of God.

Our purpose will not find us until we put aside our grandiose dream of being extraordinary people who change the world for Jesus. Our purpose is not found in some extraordinary cause or in a heroic task. Jesus longs to show us the transformative beauty of the ordinary. It grieves God when we're overly concerned with the extraordinary.

If we need a big purpose, we will end up living a small life. We will show contempt for the life we actually have and chase after the life we think we want. Yes, it can feel quite exciting for a time to be swept away in the emotional frenzy of a collective cause. We march, picket, and shout—sometimes literally, at other times metaphorically—and that makes us feel extraordinary, on the right side of history, and like we're fighting for justice. But we forget that there's a difference between being swept away by the thrill of collective enthusiasm and being filled with the Spirit of God; a difference also between the feeling of significance that comes with being a part of the herd, and the deep meaning that comes with living into our divine purpose as a unique and ordinary member of Christ's Body.

Be wary of taking on a righteous cause that feels extraordinary. It may feel good at the time, but that doesn't mean your life is giving birth to anything new and beautiful. I believe the more passionate you are about fighting, the more unlikely that God is fighting with you.

That's the problem with chasing the extraordinary. Extraordinary is always our ego's concern, and our hunger for the extraordinary usually comes from the unhealed places inside of us that haven't yet accepted acceptance and that still feel contempt for the cruciform life of waiting in weakness that Jesus offers. Indeed our purpose is never extraordinary, at least as the world defines that word. Jesus taught that giving a cup of cold water to someone in need was more than enough. It was the zeal of people who crossed land and sea to make a single convert who failed to realize God's purpose in their lives (see Matt. 23:15, 10:42).

Ordinary, Flawed, and Imperfect Moses

We cannot embrace the sacred nature of our ordinary existence unless we make peace with our flaws, defects, and vulnerabilities. Most people believe that they need to have it all together to live into their divine purpose. The Bible suggests that the opposite is true. Only flawed and vulnerable people can see the cross, accept acceptance, and wait in weakness for their purpose to reveal itself to them.

That's the paradox of living into the purpose that God has prepared for each one of us. We descend into it. As we relinquish our need to hold it all together, we tap into a divine strength that is completely at home with the ordinary fragility of human weakness.

Moses is my favorite biblical character that illustrates this principle that says God's strength is found in human weakness and vulnerability. He was among the most ordinary and flawed people that ever existed. I have heard of few people with a past as checkered as Moses's was, and his burning bush epiphany wasn't experienced in a moment of strength, but rather when Moses found himself at the end of his rope.

The Hebrew people had been enslaved in Egypt for four hundred years. Pharaoh was frightened by the rate at which the Hebrew people procreated, and so he passed a law that all newborn Hebrew boys were to be killed and thrown into the Nile River. When Moses was born, his mother couldn't stand the thought of losing him, so she hid Moses for three months from the Egyptian police. One day when she realized she couldn't hide him anymore, she made a little basket, set Moses inside, and placed the basket in the Nile River.

In an ironic twist, Pharaoh's daughter finds Moses floating along the Nile in the basket and decides to adopt him. Baby Moses is now the adopted grandson of Pharaoh himself—the king that originally wanted him dead!

Moses grows up to find that he is living in two different worlds. On the one hand, Moses is deeply concerned for the well-being of the Hebrew people. They are his flesh and blood. But on the other hand, Moses is educated, trained, and raised as Egyptian royalty. Moses lives in a palace and enjoys the delicacies that come with being among the elite. He probably even has a few servants of his own. It is hard to imagine a more dysfunctional situation: *Moses's biological family members are slaves in his own kingdom.*

Understandably, Moses has a nervous breakdown and he impulsively kills an Egyptian taskmaster. Moses is now a convicted murderer, and he is forced to flee to the land of Midian. It is in Midian that Moses begins a new life. Moses marries, has a family, and begins a new career.

After forty years of living in Midian as a refugee, God appears to Moses in the form of a burning bush. Moses has a life behind him that no one knows about. It is a life that Moses doesn't talk about, as well as a life that brings Moses great pain and shame. I can't help but imagine that it is a life that Moses has disowned altogether.

When Moses encounters God, he is fragile, weak, and his life is anything but extraordinary. It is in the midst of his ordinary life and circumstances that Moses finds his purpose. It is always in the midst of our ordinary life and circumstances that we find our purpose as well. Our purpose is not found in extraordinary circumstances, but rather in our ordinary and quite fragile circumstances.

There is something inside of us that objects to the truth that God's glory shines brightest in and through our ordinary and flawed lives. We prefer for God to work in some other way. Moses certainly did. His first response when hearing the call of God was, "Who am *I*?" (Exod. 3:11, italics mine). Moses feels far too ordinary and fragile to be used for a divine purpose. He doesn't feel special, strong, or extraordinary in any way, and Moses certainly doesn't have it all together.

Indeed one wonders if God could have chosen a more dysfunctional person to set the Hebrews free. *Think about it.* Moses has never met his parents. He is adopted. Ethnically Moses is a Hebrew, but he is raised as Egyptian royalty. He is both an enslaver of the Hebrews and an avenger of their abuse. Moses is also a coward. Not wanting to own up to his mistake, Moses runs away and begins living a lie. If this list doesn't make Moses's qualifications for leadership suspect, we later discover that Moses stutters—probably a nervous tick that developed from his dysfunctional childhood in the palace. Years of therapy could never sort it all out. Moses does not have it all together, and there is nothing extraordinary about him. That's the reason Moses objects that God could have a purpose for *his* life, and it's the same reason we object that God might have a purpose for ours as well.

We feel unworthy and just plain ordinary. We imagine God wants someone else. What we fail to see is that there is no one else, and that the Father of Jesus loves the fragility and ordinariness of the human condition. The apostle Paul writes:

> For consider your calling, brothers: not many of you were wise according to worldly standards, not many were powerful, not many were of noble birth. But God chose what is foolish in the world to shame the wise; God chose what is weak in the world to shame the strong; God chose what is low and despised in the world, even things that are not, to bring to nothing things that are, so that no human being might boast in the presence of God. (1 Cor. 1:26–29, ESV)

This is the paradox we must wrestle with as we seek to live into our purpose. Great things flow through us only as we relinquish our need to be great, and extraordinary things happen only as we embrace the miracle of our ordinary life. Thomas Merton reminds us that Christ "may exercise His power through [our] smallest and seemingly most insignificant acts."[4]

God does not delight in calling strong, talented, and extraordinary people. Rather, the people God can work with are so rooted in God's unconditional, one-way love that they actually relish their fragile and ordinary lives; they even expect God to use them for a great, albeit hidden, purpose.

Anger and Ressentiment

There is a second layer of misunderstanding that needs peeling away before our divine purpose will reveal itself to us, and that's the misguided idea that anger can aid us in living into our purpose, or that righteous anger is the fuel that drives our divine purpose. Anger is always an obstacle that prevents us from seeing our true purpose—let alone living into it. This is because anger always carries with it some level of malice. When we are angry, we want to see someone injured. We cannot be angry and bring healing to others at the same time. It is quite simply impossible and a complete and utter contradiction.

I am amazed at how people speak of anger as a good and necessary thing. It is the precursor, we think, to a more just society. But the Bible sees anger much differently—it's a cancer that plagues the human heart. Jesus taught that being angry towards another person was akin to murder (Matt. 5:22). Paul told the Ephesians that if they go to sleep angry, they leave room for Satan to wreak havoc (Eph. 4:26).

That is why a distinction must be made between feeling anger and being angry. Jesus does not prohibit us from feeling anger, but from *being* angry. Jesus emphasized the importance of never acting from an angry heart. Nor did Paul shun anger altogether. He simply said that if bedtime rolled around and our anger still lingered, it was time to let our anger go.

Anger as a feeling or a gut response is not inherently wrong or sinful. In fact, anger is a logical and sensible instinctual response to the many atrocities we see and experience in this world. The problem only comes when we act on our anger or when we take on a cause that is fueled by our anger.

One cannot see the cross, accept acceptance, and wait in weakness from a posture of anger. They are mutually exclusive life postures altogether. If we live our life in a posture of anger, the cross, unconditional acceptance, and the waiting that comes with the ordinary fragility of human life will not fuel our purpose. Put differently, we cannot take up our cause *and* take up our cross at the same time.

Our purpose reveals itself to us only as we experience inner healing, the impact of which is always to soften our anger. When anger fuels our purpose in life, we are using our purpose as a way of finding healing. But this is totally backwards. Taking up a cause will not heal the many wounds that we have suffered, let alone the wounds of others. Jesus alone can heal our wounds, whereas a righteous cause apart from Jesus will always inflict more of them.

Nietzsche used the word "ressentiment" to describe a cause that was fueled by anger. Although close to the English word resentment, the French word ressentiment involves a combination of anger, rage, woundedness, and revenge as the motivating force behind a person's cause or purpose.[5] James Hunter explains, "Ressentiment is grounded in a narrative of injury or, at least, perceived injury; a strong belief that one has been or is being wronged."[6] Anger always makes us feel like a victim. To nurse one's anger is to experience one's self as injured and to hold some person, group, or philosophy responsible for being the one to injure us.

The perception that one has been injured and that someone else is to blame is what fuels our world's violent mindset, whereby some people are victims and others are perpetrators. We then use our "righteous anger" to fuel whatever our cause happens to be. Our life mission is to lift up the victims and cast down the perpetrators. We surround ourselves with other people who tell the same story of injury, and the basis of our communion becomes nothing more than a shared narrative of how we've been wronged and a shared mission to make someone pay for it.

An extreme case of ressentiment would be the Neo-Nazis. They feel wounded, and they have a shared story as to why they are wounded, as well as a clear picture of who should be held responsible for it. As a result, their life purpose is to work against the people they perceive are responsible for injuring them. In this case, it is a particular race of people.

Consider a less extreme case of ressentiment. Amy grew up with three older siblings who were very close in age, and the second youngest child was six years Amy's senior. As a result of this age gap, Amy often found herself on the outside looking in, as her older siblings did things together that Amy could not do. This was a very painful wound that Amy experienced early on in life and that she carried with her wherever she went.

Amy watched her siblings ride roller coasters and she felt deep pain and anger that she could not participate. When her siblings all began driving, Amy stayed at home. As a young child, Amy felt excluded and left out. In fact, it wasn't too long before feeling excluded became the lens through which Amy experienced her world, a fact that wasn't helped much when she overheard her parents refer to her as their "little surprise." Though Amy was not conscious of this, over time Amy's feeling of exclusion grew into a narrative of injury. "I am not welcome and I am not wanted. There is no room for me here."

Amy took this narrative of injury with her into high school. Her two older sisters had been cheerleaders, and so Amy tried out for the squad as a freshman. Although only two freshmen make the squad annually, Amy saw her failure to make the squad as further evidence that she wasn't wanted or welcome in the world. Amy took refuge in befriending classmates that existed on the margins, and she put all of her energy into her academic work. That was the only way she could numb the pain and find the sense of welcome that she craved.

Amy's academic prowess paid off and she now attends a university where she studies political science. Amy is still unsure what she wants to do with her degree. She just knows she wants to change the world. She's pondered starting a nonprofit organization and even running for office, but at her core Amy is angry at the world's injustice and she is eager to stand up for society's excluded segment. She's ready to tackle societal problems and to do battle with whomever she thinks is keeping the marginalized people down.

Here ends my little vignette, the point of which is this: If Amy lets Jesus heal her wound of feeling excluded and unwanted, what an amazing impact she can have on the world. Her purpose will build for the Kingdom of God in a way that only she can do, and Amy will bring light and healing to those who desperately need it. Her life will be fueled by love and not by anger. Amy will be an empathic presence to those who feel unwanted and excluded. She will live as a wounded healer, as opposed to a wounded woman on a mission to experience healing through revenge.

If Amy does not relinquish herself to Jesus and find healing for her wounds and deal with the anger that flows from them, her life will in all likelihood be one experience of frustration and exclusion after another. She will subconsciously seek out experiences that leave her feeling excluded. Her real purpose in life will not be to bless the marginalized and excluded, but rather to get back at her siblings that rode the roller coaster without her and the popular girl that snickered when Amy didn't make the cheerleading squad. The tragedy of it all is that Amy will never know. She will think that she is living into her divine purpose. Anger is a cancer. Not only does it make our actions counterproductive, anger also blinds us to what is really motivating our actions in the first place.

Be wary of a person with a cause, especially if you detect that anger is fueling their cause. Be wary of taking on a cause or fighting for justice. One does not fight for justice. Rather, one becomes a vessel through which justice and healing flow. We will never live into our purpose if our anger exceeds our love and compassion.

The Truth About Our Purpose

One might be starting to sense the allusive nature of our divine purpose. No two people have the same purpose because no two people have the same mix of wounds, gifting, passion, circumstances, and social circles. There is something quite mysterious about our divine purpose.

It is worth saying that all people have a purpose. Of course, not everyone lives into his or her divine purpose. Life can certainly rob us of our purpose. We can also choose to opt out of our purpose. While our spirit yearns for purpose and adventure, our ego wants nothing more than to sabotage our divine purpose. That's because our divine purpose always kills our ego. Our ego craves safety, control, and comfort; our divine purpose, however, is about adventure, relinquishment, and being continually thrown off balance. One's purpose is allusive, which is why we make many mistakes before we find it and begin living into it. God has accounted for all of this and will one day beautify our mishaps and mistakes. But we must begin with the assertion that all people have a divine purpose.

It is equally important to state that our purpose is not to change the world. Let's not get lost in our deluded need to be extraordinary.

Changing the world is part of God's purpose. However, in living and choosing, our presence will change the *course* of this world for good or for ill. Our presence always changes the course of our families, communities, churches, and whatever other social systems we find ourselves in, for good or for ill. We can be a conduit of God's unconditional love and boundless compassion, or we can be a conduit of anger and condemnation. We cannot avoid being a conduit. Something will always flow out of us. Our presence is always moving the people around us closer to the Kingdom of God or else further away from it. Our divine purpose is the unique way that our presence brings the Kingdom of God to others.

A few other aspects of our divine purpose are worth mentioning: the necessity of healing, the value of pain, and a deep desire to be transformed.

Healing

We only live into our purpose to the extent that we let Jesus heal us. Our purpose is to become a vessel through which healing and wholeness can flow to God's broken creation. However, to become vessels of healing we must first experience it ourselves.

The healing we experience is not the removal of our wounds, but rather the *beautification* of our wounds. Even Jesus kept his wounds after he had risen from the dead. That which used to be a source of anger, shame, and resentment is beautified and transformed into a source of healing and love. The late Henry Nouwen tells us that the one "who proclaims liberation is called not only to care for his own wounds and the wounds of others, but also to make his wounds into a major source of healing power."[7]

I recently had the privilege of hearing a story of what beautified wounds look like at a luncheon keynoted by Fr. Gregory Boyle. Boyle is the author of *Tattoos on the Heart* and the founder of Homeboy

Industries. Homeboy serves high-risk men and women seeking a better alternative to gang life. Boyle's divine purpose is to help foster healthy communities, free services, and job training so that former gang members might connect with a deeper meaning.

As part of the healing process, Boyle invites the former gang members to share their stories, and on this particular occasion Boyle shared a bit about Pablo's story with us. Growing up, Pablo always wore three tee shirts. His mom beat him every day, and two tee shirts were needed to soak in the blood that flowed from the wounds. When Pablo was six, his mom asked him: "Why don't you just kill yourself?" Pablo's mom wanted nothing to do with him, and so she dropped him off at an orphanage when Pablo was nine years of age. When he went to school his classmates would laugh at Pablo for wearing three tee shirts. "Why are you wearing three tee shirts?" they asked, laughing and teasing.

Fr. Boyle told us that Pablo, when telling others about his life, always got choked up at this part of the story and began to sob. After collecting himself, Pablo spoke these words: "I wore three tee shirts because I never wanted to show people my wounds. I was ashamed of my wounds, and so I always tried to hide them. But now I see that to live into my purpose I need to welcome my wounds. How else will I ever be able to heal other people?"

Pablo's words perfectly illustrate how, by welcoming our wounds, we can live into our divine purpose. We need to be honest with ourselves and with others about the pain we have experienced and the metaphorical tee shirts we wear to make sure that no one ever sees our wounds.

Pablo experienced the healing love of Jesus. He may or may not have accepted Jesus as his Savior, and I have no clue whether or not Pablo actively attends church. That's not the point. The point is that when true healing happens, it is always a gift from the Lord as well as the doorway that leads us to discovering our divine purpose.

Pain

Finding our purpose will require a mental shift in terms of how we perceive the nature of true strength. My friend Kevin has a two-year-old son that recently concluded a prayer with these words: "I hope you have some good muscles, God!" Such is the strength that we're desperate for God to display. We want God to use his big muscles to wipe out the bad people and to vindicate the righteous, which of course always includes ourselves. But the strength we find when we see the cross is a radically different type of strength. It is something that looks a whole lot like what the world labels as weakness. In the cross we see a strength that comingles with a heavy dose of pain, uncertainty, and fear.

Paul once noted that the weakness of God was a lot stronger than human strength. He even went as far as to suggest that the weakness of God quite simply *was* divine strength.

Paul had a particularly difficult time coming to terms with this strange strength of God. In Second Corinthians, he tells a story about a "thorn in the flesh" that plagued him. We don't really know what this mysterious thorn was. Perhaps it was his poor oratory skills (2 Cor. 11:6), or maybe Paul suffered from a chronic illness that inhibited his ministry (Gal. 4:13). Whatever it was, Paul had one thorn that was just a little *too* thorny. Much like Hilary Faye, Paul wanted to be strong for Jesus. He begged God to remove the thorn from him on three separate occasions, but the only response Paul heard from God was this: "My grace is sufficient for you, for my power is made perfect in weakness."

When Paul finally grasped the strange strength of God, he was able to stop asking God to remove the source of his pain. He was even able to thank God for the gift his thorn brought with it: "I will boast all the more gladly of my weaknesses, so that the power of Christ may dwell in me" (2 Cor. 12:9). Like Pablo, Paul was able to welcome his wounds, and he came to believe that there was a divine purpose and strength behind them.

Brennan Manning tells a story that illustrates this principle perfectly in his classic book *Ruthless Trust*.[8]

A water-bearer in India had two large pots. Each hung on opposite ends of a pole that he carried across his neck. One of the pots had a crack in it, while the other was perfect. The latter always delivered a full portion of water at the end of the long walk from the stream to the master's house. The cracked pot arrived only half-full. Every day for a full two years, the water-bearer delivered only one and a half pots of water.

The perfect pot was proud of its accomplishments, because it fulfilled magnificently the purpose for which it had been made. But the poor cracked pot was ashamed of its imperfection, miserable that it was able to accomplish only half of what it had been made to do.

After the second year of what it perceived to be a bitter failure, the unhappy pot spoke to the water-bearer one day by the stream. "I am ashamed of myself, and I want to apologize to you," the pot said. "Why?" asked the bearer. "What are you ashamed of?"

"I have been able, for these past two years, to deliver only half my load, because this crack in my side causes water to leak out all the way back to your master's house. Because of my flaws, you have to do all this work and you don't get full value from your efforts," the pot said.

The bearer said to the pot, "Did you notice that there were flowers only on your side of the path, not on the other pot's side? That is because I have always known about your flaw, and I have taken advantage of it. I planted seeds on your side of the path, and every day, as we have walked back from the stream, you have watered them. For two years I have been able to pick these beautiful flowers to decorate my master's table. Without you being just the way you are, he would not have had this beauty to grace his house."

Our purpose is not something we live into by becoming a perfect pot. We live into our purpose only as we're honest and compassionate about our many cracks and the pain that comes with them, trusting that God can use our cracks to create healing in other people.

A Transformed Life

Our divine purpose is to experience personal transformation. We recall the story of the frog and the scorpion from the previous chapter. Transformation is really about two things. First, transformation happens as our stinger is softened. We become a different sort of creature altogether. Second, transformation happens as we embrace our stinger as the *thorn* that will always be with us. We know our stinger will never be fully removed in this life, and we choose to accept acceptance and show ourselves compassion because we know that God's grace is more than sufficient.

Our divine purpose is not found in some different and more extraordinary life, but rather in wholeheartedly engaging the life we do have from a place of love, vulnerability, and openness. God doesn't offer us a different life, but rather a different way of living the life that we already have.

Woody Allen once remarked that eighty percent of life is just showing up. I would add that one hundred percent of our purpose is found in learning to show up to our life in a different sort of way. We show up a bit braver, with our scars on display. We welcome our wounds, the thorns, and all the limitations we experience. We even boast in our warts and wounds as Paul did. We understand that we bring wholeness to others only as we love and accept ourselves as a cracked pot. This may sound nice, sentimental, and cute, but in fact the experience of accepting ourselves as a cracked pot is the exact opposite. It is *crucifixion through and through*—the very suffering that Jesus promises to all who heed his call.

Discussion Questions

1. Do you believe that your life has a "purpose"? If so, what is your purpose? When did you discover your purpose?

2. Do you believe Christians are called to change the world? Why or why not?

3. Do you think that being "ordinary" has a negative connotation in our culture? In what sense does our desire to be extraordinary detract from our purpose? Is a desire to be extraordinary ever a good thing?

4. What does it mean to make peace with one's flaws, defects, and vulnerabilities? Is this a desirable thing to do? Why or why not?

5. What makes you angry? Is there a difference between feeling anger and being angry? Can anger ever be a useful thing in our search to discover our divine purpose?

6. Have you ever experienced God's power in and through your weakness? If so, when? What happened and how did it impact your faith?

7. "The healing we experience is not the removal of our wounds, but rather the beautification of our wounds." Do you agree? What do beautified wounds look like? How do they relate to our purpose?

CHAPTER

5

Suffering

"It was my defeat that was to be the occasion of my rescue." —*Thomas Merton*

"All the glory when he took our place; but he took my shoulders and he shook my face. And he takes and he takes and he takes." —*Sufjan Stevens*

"Lord, how you afflict your lovers!" —*Teresa of Ávila*

have lived in Texas for most of my life, with one exception. I spent three years in northern Virginia to attend seminary. I love Virginia between mid-May and mid-September, which is precisely when I did not live there. During the academic year, it was cold. I don't mean "wear a sweater" cold. I mean wrap your body in the skin of a dead bear cold. Granted my friends from the north did not experience Virginia in quite the same way that I did, but alas, I am a native Texan. As I type these words in early December, the temperature outside is a cool seventy degrees Fahrenheit.

People say they like the winter, and I suppose some people actually do, but I am yet to meet the man who spent his working career in Florida and chose to retire in Minneapolis. When I think of winter, my mind doesn't picture a warm fire and a cup of cocoa. I think of a cold seminary dormitory room, ice, darkness, hypothermia, dead batteries, thermal underwear, depression, and recreational eating to palliate my depression.

Of course, not all of us have suffered the outer chill of a frosty climate with such despair. But eventually, for all of us, an inner cold front comes in and spiritual winter invades our soul. This experience we call suffering. It is an experience of profound loss.

Suffering is perhaps the most universal human experience. Even the healthy and wealthy amongst us eventually *lose* the things we love. We lose our spouse, our parents, our job, our hormonal balance, our purpose, or our health—and with that experience of deep loss comes a feeling of God's absence. "My God, my God," we pray with Jesus from our cross, "why have you forsaken me? Why are you so far from helping me, from the words of my groaning?" (Ps. 22:1).

But spiritual winter is more than mere loss. It is an intense fear that God is absent from our suffering, or worse, that God does not exist at all and that our suffering has no meaning. Spiritual winter is a season of bafflement, brokenness, and confusion. We pray and hear nothing but silence. No one is exempt from this experience, and we need a way of holding onto God when we fear that God is no longer holding onto us.

Job

The Book of Job is among the most heart-wrenching stories in the Bible. The Bible portrays Job as a man of integrity and faith. Job has seven sons, three daughters, a beautiful wife, lots of employees, and thousands of cattle and livestock. But in a single day Job loses everything. Job's wealth is stolen, his servants are murdered, his livestock and children die, and he develops burning sores all over his body.

Like many of us when we suffer, Job doesn't know what to do. The Bible tells us that Job goes to sit on an ash heap at the town dump and that he is utterly silent for a week. In fact, the first word Job speaks after seven days of silence is a word of lament. Enmeshed in spiritual winter, Job curses the day of his birth.

If you recall, in chapter one I stated: *The story of Job is the story of us all.* We experience our losses more slowly than Job did, but to be human is to experience the gradual loss of everything we love. In fact, so painful is this truth that we refuse to think about it because the mere thought of losing all that we love causes us so much pain. However, this experience that we're all so desperate to avoid—suffering—is actually the key to becoming more joyful and expectant disciples of Jesus. Spiritual winter is the furnace in which lovers of God and people are forged.

Suffering as Grace

Nothing inside of us wants to suffer, and yet there is nothing that will accelerate our fall into grace more than suffering. As Timothy Keller puts it, "Suffering dispels the illusion that we have strength and competence to rule our own lives and save ourselves."[1] This is precisely why suffering can be such a tremendous gift. It is a furnace with the potential to burn away every shred of self-reliance that still exists within us. Suffering takes away our need to *choose* relinquishment. Suffering relinquishes us *before* we can choose. In the midst of our suffering, our ego is murdered and we are forced to see the cross, accept acceptance, and wait in weakness in order to survive.

Several years ago a survey was conducted that asked thousands of people what one thing had the greatest impact on their spiritual development. Pain and suffering overwhelmingly clocked in as the number one answer. While it always remains true that suffering is not a part of God's Kingdom, it is equally true that God desires to use our suffering to shape us into people fit for the Kingdom. Suffering is not good, and yet God uses our suffering for tremendous spiritual good. There is no growth in the spiritual life without a willingness to suffer. Indeed the idea that we can avoid suffering is, ironically, the cause of the vast majority of our suffering. Richard Rohr points out, the "refusal of the necessary pain of being human brings to the person ten times more suffering in the long run."[2]

I do not believe that God likes suffering or that suffering causes God to smile in the same way beauty does. However, I do believe that God uses the suffering that comes with the human experience to form us into softer and humbler people.

God has an amazing capacity to use all things, especially our sin and the suffering that sin gives birth to, for our spiritual good and development. As we descend with Jesus, we increasingly experience suffering as *grace*. When life is going well and we feel nothing but God's warmth, it is impossible to relinquish ourselves fully to God. Spiritual summer always leaves us with the illusion that we are in control of our lives. When times are good, we do not see the cross and we are psychologically disconnected from the weakness that quite simply *is* the human condition. Only in the presence of pain and suffering do we get very clear about not being God. Our mind has the power to get us on our knees, but suffering alone can keep us there.

Responding to Suffering

The Christian spiritual life has more to do with unlearning than it does with learning. We hate pain and have learned an instinctual way to avoid the experience of pain, cost what it may to us or to the people we love. Freud noted that most people coming to psychotherapy did not actually want a cure for their neuroses. They just wanted relief from the pain caused by their neuroses. We hate pain and have learned clever ways to evade it.

Jesus's way of descent is about *unlearning* this avoid-pain-at-all-costs behavior. Jesus does not offer us relief from our symptoms, but rather a cure, which can only happen if we learn to embrace suffering as grace and as a gift. *There quite simply is no other way.* We experience resurrection only in proportion to our willingness to die.

A big piece of our spiritual work is to learn a new posture of heart from which to engage our suffering, which is no easy task. Americans value pleasure and personal freedom above all else, which is why we always experience suffering as traumatic and unwelcome and we are never quite sure what to do with our suffering. In fact, most people respond to suffering in one of two ways: we either stuff our pain, or else we vent our pain and externalize it in some way.

Many of us learn to stuff our pain. Rather than being honest about the pain and disillusionment that come with loss, we bury these feelings and the fear that gives birth to them in the deep places of our heart. Or as some psychologists might say, we "split off" from ourselves. I think that religious people are especially prone to stuffing their suffering because we were taught that good and faithful people shouldn't suffer. Many of us don't have room for dark and negative emotions in our spiritual worldview, and we wrongly assume that faithful people never wrestle with feelings of despair. So when suffering arises, we *bury* it deep in our heart.

The problem of course is that suffering refuses to stay buried, and we either develop physical or emotional symptoms or else we vomit the negativity and pain out in a thousand different ways. We withdraw from others, become critical of their behavior, and become more contemptuous. In the process, we lose our capacity to empathetically connect with other sufferers and even run away from them. We unconsciously refuse to see in someone else the very thing we refuse to look at in ourselves, and so we either avoid people that suffer or moralize away their suffering.

But not everyone is a stoic stuffer. Many feel the need to constantly vent their pain, or to externalize their suffering in some way. We play the role of victim, and we act and speak as if our suffering were uniquely bad and uncalled for. We verbally vomit on those who allow us to take them hostage, and we complain like a broken record about how bad off we are and about who is to blame for it. We look for others to corroborate our story of pain. We find a community glued together by mutual *ressentiment* and take turns licking one another's wounds, venting about how bad it all is, and talking about who is to blame for our suffering.

Nothing shapes our life and character more than the posture we adopt towards the suffering we experience, and tragically the suffering that God wants to use to *save us* oftentimes ends up destroying us. God wants our suffering to make us beautiful, but far too often suffering and pain can harden our souls. Suffering can be either a purifying furnace or the kiln that hardens clay. Put differently, we all experience suffering as fire. What *sort of fire* we experience suffering to be is the hinge on which our spiritual life all depends.

The Prayer of Lament

Bradley is among the most courageous young men I have ever met. I met Bradley in the early stages of his recovery from a terrible accident. Months earlier, Bradley had fallen off of a mountain when hiking and it was a miracle that he even survived. Bradley lost much of his cognitive functioning, and a full recovery of his mental faculties was unlikely. Spiritual winter had invaded Bradley's soul and, understandably, he was angry, confused, and questioning God's presence and goodness.

A breakthrough in our conversation came when Bradley realized that it was not just acceptable but encouraged for him to direct the anger and pain he felt *towards* God. I encouraged Bradley to pray with the psalmist: "Awake! Why are you sleeping, O Lord? Rouse yourself! Do not reject us forever!" (Ps. 44:23, ESV). Ultimately, it was Bradley's trust in God that allowed him to give his pain and doubt *to* God. I believe that this holy prayer of lament accelerated Bradley's emotional and spiritual recovery.

If we are forever stuffing or venting our pain, our suffering will be wasted. A new heart posture towards suffering begins when we learn to lament—to pray our suffering by directing our pain and confusion towards God. It is, after all, ultimately God that allows us to suffer. We must learn to do what Job did by finding a metaphorical ash heap from which to give our pain back to God as an offering.

The Bible is full of prayers of lament where people complain to God and even accuse God of not being honest, good, and true to God's Word. This may sound irreverent, but it is actually much healthier than stuffing and venting our pain. I suspect that God is deeply honored when we trust Him enough to take the suffering we are given and question the only One that actually has the power to take it away and who chooses not to. Complaining to God may sound irreverent, but it is actually the beginning of what I will call the "formed life."

The Formed Life: From Lament to Embrace

A great shift takes place in the Christian spiritual life when we move away from our instinctual drive to avoid suffering and adopt a posture of wholehearted embrace. This is not the same as exercising our willpower and taking up our cross, but about saying "yes" to the experience of Jesus's cross taking us up. We see suffering as God's grace because it takes from us what our stubborn will refuses to give up: the illusion of control.

A headier theological grasp of God's grace will never move us to relinquish our self to the purposes of God, nor does a cognitive apprehension of grace teach us to love weakness, which, according to the Bible, is the only place that God's power can be experienced. Suffering alone can break our addiction to control. Only from our inner ash heap do we learn the art of waiting in weakness for God to resurrect us. We come to see suffering as the refiner's fire that alone can make us more like Jesus, who the Bible speaks of as "a man of sorrows and acquainted with grief" (Isa. 53:3, ESV).

Larry Crabb of New Way Ministries offers an insightful image as to how suffering forms us for God's Kingdom.[3] Consider the familiar image of an iceberg (see Figure 5.1). Our instinctual preference is to live at the tip of the iceberg, which Crabb calls "the managed life." In this particular paradigm of faith, suffering is grace when we allow it to drive us into our own inner depths, which is where we find Jesus and experience transformation.

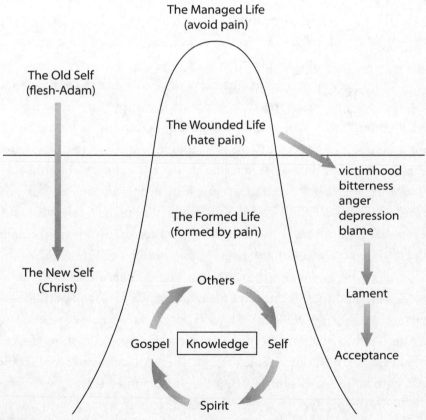

Figure 5.1

The Managed Life

We instinctually prefer to spend our lives at the tip of the iceberg, which is where the illusion of control is held firmly intact. Here we find ourselves desperate to captain our own ship and author our own script. It is what Paul refers to as "the old man"—a part of us that is a lie or a "false self" because it has already been crucified with Christ.

When I live a managed life, I am not actually *in* control. It is only the illusion of control that is strong. We see the managed life in people that want to bargain with God. To think that God needs anything from us at all or that we have even a chip with which to bargain with God is a spiritual error of massive proportion. Developmentally, such a worldview is appropriate for a child, but as Paul put it so well: "When I was a child, I spoke like a child, I thought like a child, I reasoned like a child. When I became a man, I gave up childish ways" (1 Cor. 13:11, ESV).

Nothing reveals the managed life within us more than the mental shock and horror that often accompanies our experience of suffering. We wonder: "Why would God let this happen to *me*? I haven't done anything wrong!" Such statements, though perhaps part of a normal grief process, are utterly staggering in their theological blindness. It takes little mental effort to grasp just how deep, random, and disproportionately distributed suffering is across the planet. But when suffering happens to *me*, something has gone terribly wrong, especially when we're convinced that we have done nothing to "deserve" it.

This is the essence of the managed life: a belief that we get what we deserve and that because we manage our life in a way that doesn't harm others (or so we think), we *deserve* a pain-free existence. This is utterly mind boggling from the perspective of the Christian Gospel, which makes no bones about its consistent promise that we should *expect* to suffer (see John 15:18; 1 Pet. 4:12; James 1:2).

Many people live a managed life well into their "senior" years, never having truly "grown up." People who maintain this top-of-the-iceberg existence either have suffered very little, or else their heart is so layered in protective armor that life has not taken their illusion of control away from them. There is a massive trade-off we experience in living the managed life. On the one hand, we suffer less. The armor that layers our heart shields us from the experience of vulnerability, and the scales on our eyes keep alive the illusion that we are in control of our destiny. We *experience* the managed life as a good thing, though in fact it is not good at all. The managed life is, by definition, a shallow life and a surface life, which is why in choosing to suffer less, we at the same time *love less* and often become loveless as a result.

Eventually, we must all let go of the managed life. Even if relinquishment is not a value we hold, suffering simply *will take away* our illusion of control from us. When our spouse leaves, our children disappoint us, our body fails us, retirement bores us, or death knocks on our door, the pain of that experience will drive us down to the next necessary stage in our fall into grace: the wounded life.

The Wounded Life

Here we find people in deep pain and confusion. Their illusion of control has been taken from them, but their *desire* for control has not changed. This is where feelings of victimhood, bitterness, anger, and depression live. We are very present to our own unique suffering, which we view as unfair. We feel as if our suffering were no doubt worse than everyone else's suffering. For the Christian, this is where the prayer of lament begins.

Many people in today's world live the "wounded life." We see the wounded life in people who prefer to live disappointed rather than having the occasional experience of disappointment. Furthermore, people stuck living a wounded life have no more capacity for love than people living a managed life, as love, from the Christian perspective, always includes a willingness to suffer for the sake of the beloved. Wounded souls may experience more *connection* than isolated managed selves, but the source of that connection is usually some form of *ressenti-ment*. There is a narrative of injury, albeit an unstated and uncon-scious one, that binds wounded souls. Shared pain and a common understanding that life has robbed us of our due is the glue that binds us together. I suppose this is a better existence than the managed life, but only in the sense that eating dog food is "better" than eating dirt. Neither constitutes the feast that we were created to taste. Richard Rohr puts it quite well in *Falling Upward*:

> It has been acceptable for some time in America to remain "wound identified" (that is, using one's victimhood as one's identity, one's ticket to sympathy, and one's excuse for not serving), instead of using the wound to "redeem the world," as we see in Jesus and so many people who turn their wounds into sacred wounds that liber-ate both themselves and others.[4]

The wounded life is especially dangerous when our cherished memories of suffering become the crux of our identity. It is far too common to build a self-understanding around the dark moments that we experience. David Benner borrows Eckhart Tolle's language and refers to someone stuck in the wounded life as a pain body. "This pain body," he says, "needs to be fed to remain alive, and it does this by seeking out and experiencing more pain."[5] Whenever we allow an inner narrative of victimhood to rule within us for too long, we actu-ally become the story we tell about ourselves and even *unconsciously act in ways that will create realities that support our story*. Our story of victimhood creates our life much more than it describes it, which is a frightening thought.

It is hard to conceive why anyone would cling to an identity rooted in pain and victimhood, but that people so frequently do forces us to give an account for why this is so. Thomas Joiner is very helpful in his book *Lonely at the Top*. He points out that our need for self-verification, which is the safe and familiar knowledge of how we view ourselves and how others view us, often outweighs our desire to change *even when* our sense of self is incredibly painful and unmanageable. We would rather our thoughts, words, and actions verify a self we do not like than risk the chaos of losing the only self we know. He uses the example of bulimic people who, though they hate who they are, nevertheless cannot change who they are. He writes:

> A self-verification perspective would suggest the intriguing possibility that bulimic people, in an effort to meet self-verification needs, structure interpersonal discourse in such a way that negative views about the physical self—which by all accounts are quite painful to them—are stabilized and perpetuated.[6]

Translation: our need to verify who we imagine ourselves to be, or our need for a clear identity, is so great that we would rather be a wounded and bleeding self than to risk having *no* self at all. The tragedy of it all is that there is, from the Christian perspective, a magnificent self to be discovered—a self that is hidden with Christ in God which we discover *only in proportion* to our willingness to die (Col. 3:3). It is precisely this realization that a true self exists that has the capacity to alter our relationship with suffering. That there *is* a self that is hidden in the Divine, which is not at all the same as the "I" my ego "knows," enables us to see suffering as *grace that drives us down into our own inner depths where Christ and the true me lives*. It is this *metanoia*, or shift of the mind, that enables us to see suffering as grace that accelerates the formed life.

The Formed Life

I do not believe that we will ever like suffering, nor is it ever appropriate to rejoice at the suffering of another person. Indeed part of our call as Christians is to eliminate as much suffering as we can from other people's lives. I am not trying to sell you on something here that

I myself don't believe—namely, that suffering is good or not as bad as you think. Suffering is *worse* than you think. Otherwise, God wouldn't have a plan to banish suffering from creation once and for all.

My interest is merely in changing how we experience our suffering. I flat out assume that, until Christ returns in glory, all humans will suffer, and it is simply a waste of time to pine away in pain and pity wishing it were otherwise. This is especially true since God wills to use our suffering to form us for good (Rom. 3:5; Job 23:10; James 1:2). Suffering is a furnace that can burn away every ounce of self-reliance that exists within us. Suffering may be a theological problem, but God is resourceful and creative, and God *wills to use the "problem" of suffering as the key ingredient in God's solution.* God doesn't just casually defeat death. God spits in the face of suffering by using death to overcome death. For this reason, as we relinquish ourselves to the will of God, suffering becomes grace that drives us down into our own depths. It is precisely here in our own inner depths, deep beneath the iceberg of our conscious, shallow, and managed existence, that we encounter God and our deepest self and experience transformation.

Only in our depths do we come to *know* God or our self for the first time. Until now we have only known God as a concept or as a projection of our own inner fears and hopes. Nor until now have we really known our self. All our lives we have been attached to a name, a role, an achievement, or a wound. But as we allow the grace of suffering to drive us down into our own inner depths, the self we have constructed is burned away and we meet our true self for the first time.[7]

In our depths we also experience a changed relationship with *knowledge*, which until now we have largely seen as a head game. We used to think knowledge was about having the right facts—about God, the world, and ourselves. It's not that we now despise this rational way of knowing, but in our depths we *transcend* this particular way of knowing. We begin to know God and ourselves in a much different way. In our depths knowing becomes increasingly experiential, intimate, wordless, and sexual. This form of knowing the Hebrew people understood quite well, as their word for knowing was a synonym for sexual intercourse. We will have much more to say about this transrational way of knowing in chapter seven.

As the grace of suffering drives us down into our depths, we experience increasing *knowledge*, or perhaps soul experience, around four different aspects of life. When we live the formed life, we increase our heart knowledge of (1) other people, (2) ourselves, (3) the Holy Spirit, and (4) the Christian Gospel. We will explore each of these themes in the next chapter since the transparent sharing of what *we know* to be true about other people, the Holy Spirit, the Gospel, and ourselves is the heart of evangelism. We will speak more of this later, but for now note that true evangelism is not a clever mental exercise, but rather an interpersonal experience that flows quite naturally from our depths.

Knowledge of the Other

The great irony of our descent into self is that for the first time we come to know other people, even those whom we have never met, in a more intimate way. In touching our own deep and suffering self, we can now access the suffering of all humanity. The deeper we go into self, the fewer strangers we encounter. Our deep knowledge of other people produces within us compassion and empathy. Suddenly we *know*, again in a way that transcends the rational mind, that it is not just we who struggle and suffer, but that all of us are struggling, too.

Knowledge of the Self

John the Seer speaks of "a white stone, with a new name written on the stone that no one knows except the one who receives it" (Rev. 2:17, ESV). It is precisely *this stone* that we receive as we fall into grace and meet our true self, or what Richard Rohr calls our immortal diamond. We see a pearl of great price within, albeit in a mirror dimly, and in our joy we sell all that we have to purchase that pearl. Until now we had not even considered that there was a self that transcended my thoughts, roles, feelings, and achievements.

Knowledge of the Spirit

It becomes increasingly hard to desire control when we know that a Benevolent and Wise Spirit orders all things for our good. A life lived from our depths becomes lighter. We increasingly relinquish our need to change the world, ourselves, or other people. We cease to fear the chaos when we know the Spirit that hovers over it and orders the chaos for good (see Gen. 1:2).

Knowledge of the Gospel

The descent into our depths burns away whatever shred of do-it-yourself religion that still exists within us. There no longer exists room for pride or judgment. We *know* "all have sinned and fall short of the glory of God, and are justified by his grace as a gift" (Rom. 3:23–24, ESV). Our spiritual life is now to be a continual opening up of that gift, and a sharing of the gift of God's grace from our depths with other people.

Formative Suffering

A great shift occurs in the Christian spiritual life when we come to see our suffering as the key to becoming more like Jesus. When God's Kingdom arrives in its fullness, spiritual winter will be abolished once and for all. But in the meantime, spiritual winter has a role to play in our fall into grace.

In the presence of suffering, we get very clear about not being God. Most of us interpret our suffering as evidence of God's absence, but I would argue that the exact opposite is true. Suffering can be a sign that God is working in our life. Oftentimes when we most feel that God is trying to kill us, God is actually in the final mile of saving us.

Martin Luther made a distinction between theologians of glory and theologians of the cross, the latter of which alone could properly be called theologians. Whereas theologians of glory are always articulating schemes by which we might ascend to God, a theologian of the cross sees all of our trials, suffering, guilt, confusion, and troubles as *God's doing*. The point of faith is not to see through our suffering, to ponder how we might solve it, or to pray for God to take it away. Our suffering rather comes directly from God's hand, and its purpose is to draw us into the cross story. Suffering is always meant to kill us so that we might be made alive again.

The theologian of the cross, Luther said, has no interest in becoming a "good" person. He sees our pursuit to become good as a vain neurosis of the managed life. His spiritual work is to die with Jesus and to await God's answer *in* Him—to see the cross, accept acceptance, and wait in weakness for resurrection from death.

Rethinking Spiritual Formation

One of my tasks as a Christian minister is to help people and churches think deeply about spiritual formation, both what it is and how it happens in our lives. I notice that many people with an interest in spiritual formation talk about programs and practices, but that few, if any, talk about our *need* to suffer as part of any meaningful spiritual transformation. I believe suffering is necessary and when we seek to evade the necessary suffering of being human, we end up bringing ten times more suffering to the people we love and ourselves in the long run.[8]

Luther's great gift is to see spiritual formation through the lens of the cross. We are not spiritually formed by evading the cross, and the goal of the spiritual life is not to share in Jesus's sufferings *less*. Transformation is about taking the sufferings of Christ into our heart more. As Paul put it, we fill up in our flesh what is lacking in Christ's afflictions for the sake of the Church (Col. 1:24).[9]

Luther described the formed life as a repetitive and mutually interpretive dance of *oratio* (the prayer of desire), *meditatio* (meditation on the Word of God), and *tentatio* (spiritual affliction, trial, and temptation). It is our experience of *tentatio*—suffering, pain, want, affliction, trial, fear, uncertainty, and guilt—that drives us to *meditatio* so that we might make meaning of our suffering. This leads to *oratio*, which is a deep soul prayer to God whereby we yearn for wholeness and reconciliation. We find that the more we desire God (*oratio*), the more we experience *tentatio*—inner and outer suffering. It is this repetitive and mutually interpretive dance, or this never-ending cycle of *oratio*, *meditatio*, and *tentatio*, that grace uses to drive us down into our own inner depths (see Figure 5.2). Apart from a necessary suffering, the formed life is not possible. In his 1532 table talks, Luther put it like this:

> I did not learn my theology all at once, but had to search constantly deeper and deeper for it. My temptations did that for me, for no one can understand Holy Scripture without practice and temptations. That is what the enthusiasts and sects lack. They don't have the right critic, the devil, who is the best teacher of theology. If we don't have that kind of devil, then we become nothing but speculative theologians, who do nothing but walk around in our own thoughts and speculate with our reason alone as to whether things should be like this, or like that.[10]

We could all wish that we did not have to suffer, and we can waste precious spiritual time whining about the fact that we do have to suffer. But there comes a point in our fall into grace when God asks us not just to accept suffering but to also *embrace* its redemptive purpose in our life. Otherwise, we live our lives stuck in a wounded existence, forever looking for someone to blame for our pain or for someone to take it away. *But in this life the pain is not going away.* To quote Rohr once more: "Do not waste a moment of time lamenting poor parenting, lost job, failed relationship, physical handicap, gender identity, economic poverty, or even the tragedy of any kind of abuse. *Pain is part of the deal.*"[11]

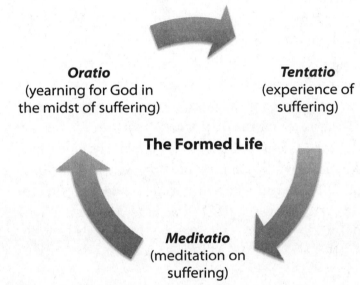

Oratio
(yearning for God in
the midst of suffering)

Tentatio
(experience of
suffering)

The Formed Life

Meditatio
(meditation on
suffering)

Figure 5.2

For the Sake of the World

Coming from a Eucharistic tradition, I have come to realize that a Christian is like communion bread. We are first and foremost taken and blessed by God. However, the taking and blessing only constitutes the first half of the sacrament. The taking and blessing is a prelude to the second and more glorious half—the *breaking* and the *giving out.* Like the communion bread and like the Lord who's Body it signifies, we are taken and blessed so that God might *break us* and give us out.

In this chapter we have largely been looking at the breaking, the suffering that is necessary for us to live the formed life. We have seen how pain alone can drive us deep into our depths where our true and hidden self is to be found. However, we never suffer for our sake alone, but as Alexander Schmemann noted, "for the life of the world." As the Psalmist notes, "Deep calls to deep" (Ps. 42:7). Only as we descend into our inner depths can we lovingly nudge people down with us into the depths of God's love and grace, which is the very essence of evangelism.

If you read these words amidst a spiritual summer, I am deeply glad for you. That is where my own soul finds itself, which is perhaps the only reason I have the strength and perspective to write these words on suffering. If, on the other hand, you are lost in spiritual winter, make no effort as Merton says "to escape from the heat of the fire that is meant to soften and prepare you to become your true self."[12] Take the suffering from God's hand as grace, and allow it to drive you down beyond a wounded existence into your own inner depths. There you will find not only God but your true self, and a Voice crying inward: "Take heart; get up, he is calling you" (Mark 10:49).

Discussion Questions

1. What does the phrase "spiritual winter" mean to you? Have you ever experienced it? What happened and how did the situation resolve itself?

2. Do you believe that God willingly allows us to suffer? Do you believe that God wants to use suffering for good?

3. What is your default response to the experience of suffering? For instance, do you vent your pain, stuff your pain, or perhaps do something else?

4. Do you think it is irreverent to direct your anger at God when you suffer? Why or why not?

5. What role has suffering played in your own spiritual journey? Is there any sense in which suffering has deepened your faith?

6. In what sense are you currently living the "managed life"? The "wounded life"? The "formed life"? Is it possible to live all three at the same time?

7. Have you ever explored your own "inner depths"? What does that phrase mean to you, and how do we "descend" into our depths?

CHAPTER

6

Evangelism

"How beautiful upon the mountains are the feet of him who brings good news, who publishes peace, who brings good news of happiness, who publishes salvation." —*Isaiah 52:7 (ESV)*

"But you will receive power when the Holy Spirit has come upon you; and you will be my witnesses in Jerusalem, in all Judea and Samaria, and to the ends of the earth." —*Acts 1:8*

"Preach the Gospel always, and when necessary, use words." —*Francis of Assisi*

veryone remembers his or her favorite babysitter growing up. Mine was Caroline. I remember Caroline being really into Jesus, and she always seemed eager to talk to my siblings and me about God. Of course, the feeling was mutual as I was never without questions and thoughts of my own.

I recall that when I was about five years old, Caroline told me that Jesus loved me and that he died to erase my sins. I think I had just spilled my juice box on the carpet and I was feeling pretty guilty about the whole thing, and so I was ripe to hear a message about God's unconditional love and forgiveness. Caroline explained that it didn't matter how many juice boxes I spilled because Jesus died to undo my silly mistakes and that nothing I did could ever separate me from the one-way love of Jesus.

I recall that my first instinct as a child was to share this incredible news, and so I looked at Caroline with all the intensity I could muster and I asked her the question that was pressing upon my heart: "Does Suzie know this?"

Suzie was my best friend and my kindergarten compatriot; I told Suzie everything. As a result, if Suzie had not yet heard the good news about Jesus, I reasoned that it was my job to tell her. So the next day at school I cornered Suzie by the monkey bars at recess and I told her the good news about Jesus.

I don't really remember what happened next. I think the bell rang and we all enthusiastically ran back indoors to finger paint. However, it does remind me that growth into spiritual adulthood happens only as we reconnect with the lost and fragmented pieces of our inner spiritual child, a part of us that understands that some news is so good that we are compelled to share it with others.

Can I Get a Witness?

We would be wrong to assume that evangelism is some arbitrary technique or principle that we undertake to share the Gospel, grow the Church, or even change the world. Authentic evangelism is connected to our deepest self and flows organically from our inner depths. It happens naturally as we fall into grace and descend with Jesus into a more relinquished and free existence. Evangelism happens as we reconnect to that child within that cannot *not* share what it knows to be true.

We recall that our fall into grace begins, ends, and is sustained by the one-way love of God, which Christians call grace. Our experience of grace grows as we see the cross, accept acceptance, and wait in weakness. It is this circular and repetitive process that empowers us to take baby steps to bear our suffering in community and relinquish our illusion of being in control. This process of descent is inherently healing. We not only discover the source of our wounds, but we also discover that our divine purpose flows *from* our wounds. Our wounds are transformed into sacred wounds. This epiphany completely changes how we understand and experience suffering. How then does evangelism organically flow from this experience of descending into the formed life?

> *We bear witness to the love of Jesus Christ by being transparent, both in word and deed, about the manner in which grace, relinquishment, healing, purpose, and profound meaning in the midst of suffering is the bedrock of our spiritual life.*

Philip and the Eunuch

The word *witness* is at the heart of biblical evangelism, and it is a word that conveys a posture of both showing and telling. Witnessing is primarily about telling and about using words to put flesh on what we know to be true from experience. For instance, if we see a car crash and the case goes before a judge, we may be called in as a witness.

But the word witness is also about showing. The Greek word translated witness is *martus*, which is where we get the word martyr. The first Christians bore witness to their love for Jesus and Jesus's love for them in and through their courageous willingness to suffer and die for the Gospel. Their death evangelized the world as it bore witness to their faith in Jesus. As the old adage goes, actions speak louder than words.

There is a story in the Bible that perfectly captures this balance of showing and telling that lies at the heart of evangelism. It is about a disciple named Philip and an African eunuch whose name we do not know. It is a beautiful story and very much worth quoting at length.

> Now an angel of the Lord said to Philip, "Rise and go toward the south to the road that goes down from Jerusalem to Gaza." This is a desert place. And he rose and went. And there was an Ethiopian, a eunuch, a court official of Candace, queen of the Ethiopians, who was in charge of all her treasure. He had come to Jerusalem to worship and was returning, seated in his chariot, and he was reading the prophet Isaiah. And the Spirit said to Philip, "Go over and join this chariot." So Philip ran to him and heard him reading Isaiah the prophet and asked, "Do you understand what you are reading?" And he said, "How can I, unless someone guides me?" And he invited Philip to come up and sit with him. Now the passage of the Scripture that he was reading was this: "Like a sheep he was led to the slaughter and like a lamb before its shearer is silent, so he opens not his mouth. In his humiliation justice was denied him. Who can describe his generation? For his life is taken away from the earth." And the eunuch said to Philip, "About whom, I ask you, does the prophet say this, about himself or about someone else?" Then Philip opened his mouth, and beginning with this Scripture he told him the good news about Jesus. And as they were going along the road they came to some water, and the eunuch said, "See, here is water! What prevents me from being baptized?" And he commanded the chariot to stop, and they both went down into the water, Philip and the eunuch, and he baptized him. And when they came up out of the water, the Spirit of the Lord carried Philip away, and the eunuch saw him no more, and went on his way rejoicing. But Philip found himself at Azotus, and as he passed through he preached the gospel to all the towns until he came to Caesarea. (Acts 8:26–40, ESV)

This biblical story perfectly illustrates the deep interconnection between experiencing Jesus and sharing Jesus. Whenever we authentically descend with Jesus into the depths of God's love and into the depths of our true self, we cannot help but pull others down with us so that they too experience God and themselves in a deeper and more meaningful way. We do not experience grace, relinquish our lives to God, find healing, discover our divine purpose, and embrace suffering for our own private and spiritual edification. *We descend with Jesus for the sake of the world.* As we fall into grace, God intends that we lovingly pull others down with us into the depths of God's one-way love. This is precisely what it means to bear witness to the Living Christ, which always requires four things: we must (1) know a person's story, (2) know ourselves, (3) know the Spirit, and (4) know the Gospel (see Figure 6.1). We recall from the previous chapter that this "knowledge" is imparted only as we live the formed life and experience suffering as grace that drives us deep into our depths, which in Christ becomes a bottomless reservoir of truth.

Figure 6.1

Know Their Story

We have all had the experience of thinking that we knew a person only to realize that we mistook our assumptions, stereotypes, and unconscious biases about them for the truth of their being. Personally, I have had this experience far too many times! I am learning to engage people from a deep place of curiosity and openness. I fail at this more often than I succeed, but on my best days I truly believe that each person is a miracle and I engage them with an open heart hoping to learn something about their unique story.

There is always so much more to a person than what meets the eye. On the surface, one might assume that there is not much we can know about this eunuch. After all, the Bible doesn't even give us his name. But there is actually a lot we can infer about this eunuch if we just do a little digging.

We can infer that this eunuch is powerful and that he has sacrificed a lot to get to the top. In Western culture, we tend to measure our sense of self by what we possess and achieve. This eunuch, however, comes from a more traditional culture where a man's value and identity was tied to his family. But this eunuch can't have a family because he has been castrated, a requirement for commoners that wanted to serve in the royal court. So we can reasonably infer that this eunuch is rich and powerful, but that he has also sacrificed a lot to get his money and power.

There is also evidence to suggest that this eunuch is incredibly hollow inside and that he longs for a deep and meaningful experience of God. He has climbed the royal ladder only to find a big heap of emptiness waiting for him at the top. Everything this eunuch imagined would make him happy—the power, the influence, the education, the prestige, and the money—they just haven't delivered. So the eunuch packs his bags and travels 1,600 miles from Ethiopia to Jerusalem on a spiritual wild goose chase to worship in the Jewish

Temple. In biblical times this was a long and dangerous journey, but the eunuch rolls the dice because he has nothing to lose. Everything he has worked so hard to attain for himself and the many sacrifices have left him hollow. "Jerusalem," he says, "here I come."

Finally, because Philip encounters this eunuch on his way back from Jerusalem, we can infer that this eunuch is a mental and emotional wreck. The Book of Deuteronomy clearly states that eunuchs are not welcome in the Temple. So after months of traveling, this eunuch would have arrived in Jerusalem only to be dismissed. *People like him weren't allowed in.* Imagine how rejected, unwanted, and unclean this eunuch must have felt when he met Philip on the road.

I wonder where the eunuch's story resonates with your own. After all, we all have a story of pain, heartbreak, and betrayal, as well as a unique set of fears, joys, dreams, and wounds that only the Gospel can address. Each person has a unique spiritual autobiography; only as we get to know a person's story does our capacity to witness to them grow.

Authentic evangelism is slow, organic, and dependent on having a meaningful relationship with another person. We speak the Gospel into a person's story only as we have earned the right to hear their story in a deep and meaningful way over time. We don't corner people by the monkey bars and shove Jesus down their throat. Authentic evangelism is a lot riskier and more organic than that. It happens as we take down our walls and let the Jesus in us both find and be found by the Jesus that's hiding in the depths of someone else.

We cannot witness to someone apart from a meaningful relationship with them. We can share our ideas about Jesus with people we do not know, but *sharing Jesus* with someone works differently. Sharing Jesus, or witnessing, is a vulnerable and risky process through and through and it happens only as two people get to know one another.

We all carry within us a deep and instinctual need to be seen and heard. Before we share Jesus with someone else, we must first get to know them. Before we open our mouth, we first open our heart and our ears. We don't just hop into someone's chariot and start sharing the Gospel uninvited. The first step is always to run alongside their chariot for a while like Philip did and to get to know the person that's inside.

Truly getting to know someone can take a lot of time, and it often requires tremendous patience and faith. But at the same time the patient work of building a relationship with someone is not optional if we want to do the work of evangelism. We cannot make the mistake of assuming that a person's public persona is a true representation of who they are. For instance, on the outside this eunuch is powerful, accomplished, intelligent, and rich, but on the inside he is suffering. I believe this is how most people experience life. Life is hard and at times a deep struggle. We may be very skilled at putting on our brave face, but on the inside we hurt and we experience suffering. Our default instinct might be to blame someone for our suffering, but I have learned that the deepest part of our self longs to experience meaning and intimacy *in the midst* of our pain. Indeed it is usually a lack of authentic connection with others that generates our experience of suffering.

We do not bear witness to the love of Jesus Christ in a vacuum, but rather to hurting people in the unique circumstances of their lives. Remember, before we hop into someone's chariot and start reading from our scroll, we must first run alongside them for a while. We build a relationship. We discern what's under their façade, the places they've been hurt, and how the world has rejected them and made them feel unclean.

However, we do not get to know someone's story as a means to the end of sharing the Gospel. In the Christian life there is nothing instrumental about relationship. It is not that we have "a Gospel to share" but to do that work we must first build relationships. On the contrary, true evangelism sees relationship as inherently valuable and knows that God longs to speak a fresh word to us in and through the very people to whom the Spirit invites us to witness. Nevertheless, our first assignment as witnesses to Jesus Christ is always to get to know someone and to join their chariot. That then leaves them with the choice of whether or not to invite us in.

Know Yourself

If we truly want to bear witness to the one-way love of Jesus Christ, it is not enough to get to know other people. We must also get to know ourselves at a much deeper and more intimate level. We must become the sort of person other people want with them in their chariot.

We can only be a vessel of transformation to the extent that we have experienced transformation and we extend grace to others only as we experience grace in ourselves. When grace fills our heart, we find it psychologically impossible to judge another person. If our spiritual task is to see the cross, accept acceptance, and to wait in weakness, there is quite literally no room in our heart for judgment. We recall that authentic witness, or biblical evangelism, is about telling and *showing*. This implies that just as important as the message we share is the character of the one sharing the news. We must be the sort of person others want with them in their chariot: joyful, safe, authentic, vulnerable, generous, and nonjudgmental above all else.

I find it interesting that the Holy Spirit urges Philip to *join* the eunuch's chariot, but that the Spirit doesn't instruct Philip to jump inside. Only the eunuch can issue the invitation "in," which is always where evangelism happens.

The Spirit may urge us to invest in a particular relationship, but for any meaningful evangelism to take place, that person must be the one to invite us *inside* the chariot of their unique story. Knowing ourselves is crucial. God invites us to see those parts of our own inner life that might be barriers to other people inviting us in. For instance:

Maybe we're shallow.

Maybe we're cynical.

Maybe we have a low tolerance for mystery and mess.

Maybe we have a way of always bringing it back to us.

Maybe we're bad listeners.

Maybe we're fixers.

Maybe we use people.

Maybe we're arrogant.

Maybe we're angry.

Maybe we're controlling.

Maybe we theologize away people's pain.

Maybe we don't walk our talk.

Maybe we don't love people.

Or maybe you've been reading this list and thinking, "That sounds just like my spouse, coworker, or my daughter." It is so easy to see the speck in someone else's eye, but it takes great courage to look at the log jammed in our own. This is precisely what a commitment to self-knowledge is all about. We commit to seeing the log in our own eye, and we trust that as we see the cross, accept acceptance, and wait in weakness that God will remove it.

The reason a relentless self-focus is so crucial is because at the heart of meaningful evangelism is empathy. Empathy isn't over-identification. Empathy isn't what happens when your trauma traumatizes me, or when the line between your story and mine gets blurred. On the contrary, empathy happens when we listen deeply to another person's story and can see things from their perspective and connect with their experience. Yes their story may be different, but it's not alien to our experience. We understand the underlying emotions that drive someone's story of pain, for a deep self-knowledge gives us access to those same human emotions in ourselves. Empathy happens whenever we can listen to another person's story and say, "Me, too. I have access to something of your experience. I know this darkness in my own heart and you are not alone. I know your doubt, your fear, and your guilt. *Me, too.*"

I like to think that Philip was invited into the eunuch's chariot because Philip could empathize with the eunuch's desire for rescue and healing. Perhaps Philip had never climbed the royal ladder only to find emptiness at the top or been barred from entering the Temple. In fact, one might easily assume that Philip has nothing in common with this eunuch, as they are of a different race and religion. But I believe empathy got Philip a ticket inside the eunuch's chariot because empathy is the only thing that gets any of us invited in.

There is no evangelism without a commitment to knowing ourselves, for authentic self-knowledge gives us access to the experience of others. Of course, evangelism shouldn't be reduced to a human technique or strategy. We recall that witnessing is always a supernatural phenomenon. It is not enough to know ourselves and other people. We must also get deeply acquainted with the Spirit of God.

Know the Spirit

The most important detail of Philip's encounter with the Ethiopian is that God is the architect of the experience from beginning to end. The Spirit tells Philip to join the eunuch's chariot, and when the encounter ends, the Spirit carries Philip off to his next assignment. At no point does Philip seize the initiative. Rather Philip *is* seized by a force much greater than himself, and he merely participates in what the Spirit of God is already doing. When it comes to evangelism, the same always holds true for us.

Evangelism doesn't happen when we roll up our sleeves, exercise our will, seize the initiative, and bear witness to Jesus Christ. Instead we grow in our willingness to follow the Spirit's lead and in our capacity to hear the Spirit's Voice. Christians believe that God is always on the scene long before we are. It isn't our job to use our intellect and cleverness to persuade someone to make a decision for Christ. It is always the Spirit of God that woos people into the arms of Jesus. We simply have the privilege of being a willing participant.

Whenever we feel called to share the love of Jesus with another person, we always begin by looking for how God is *already* at work in their lives. We discern traces of grace that are already present. We look for what God has already set in motion that we want to participate in. Before we ever say a word, we first open our ears. We listen, look, and pray so that the Spirit might involve us in *God's* work.

Eventually the time will come for us to open our mouths and speak, which can feel scary, vulnerable, and risky. The Bible indeed urges us to "honor Christ the Lord as holy, always being prepared to make a defense to anyone who asks you for a reason for the hope that is in you" (1 Pet. 3:15, ESV). When grace, relinquishment, healing, purpose, and meaning in the midst of suffering are the bedrock of our spiritual life, people simply *will* ask us about our experience of God. We'll be invited inside the chariot of people's lives if we live the way of descent with any integrity. To give an account for the hope that is in us we must be well acquainted with the language of the Spirit.

Eugene Peterson notes that there are three types of language. First, there is *descriptive* language. The purpose of descriptive language is to name what is there. It is language *about* and its goal is to orient us in reality. Descriptive language gives us a framework so that we do not get lost. The Bible uses a lot of descriptive language: God is merciful. God was born of the Virgin Mary. God forgives our sins. This is all descriptive language about God and about the spiritual life.

The second type of language is *motivational* language. This type of language uses words to get things done. Commands are issued, requests are made, and promises are offered. It doesn't matter whether we choose to motivate people with threats or with candy;

the purpose of motivational language is to persuade someone to move. Jesus used this type of language, too. "Store up for yourselves treasure in heaven. Seek first the Kingdom of God. Repent!" This is all motivational language.

Descriptive language and motivational language are both important, but neither one is of primary importance when it comes to being a graceful evangelist because neither type of language is the primary language of the Spirit. The primary language of the Spirit is *personal language*.

According to Eugene Peterson, personal language "uses words to express oneself, to converse, to be in relationship. This is language to and with. Love is offered and received, ideas are developed, feelings are articulated, and silences are honored. This is . . . a language that is unhurried, unforced, unexcited—the leisurely language of friends and lovers, which is also the language of prayer."[1] Personal language is mysterious and intimate and vulnerable and life changing. It's the kind of language that can only happen *inside the chariot*.

Paul says the Spirit of God intercedes for each one of us with sighs too deep for words, an example of personal language. Personal language is when my wife looks at me and says "timshel" because that particular word has meaning inside the chariot of our marriage. Personal language is Paul's cry, "I have been crucified with Christ; and it is no longer I who live, but Christ who lives in me. And the life I now live in the flesh I live by faith in the Son of God, who loved me and gave himself for me" (Gal. 2:19–20). Now *that* is personal language.

People will say they can't be a witness to Christ because they don't know enough about the Bible or how to refute the claims of atheism. They wrongly assume that a witness is like a good attorney that cleverly knows how to argue God's case. But this is to totally misunderstand what it means to be a witness. Some people are called to *describe* the Kingdom of God in a compelling way, and perhaps even to *motivate* others to give their life to Christ. *But that's not what witnessing is!*

Graceful evangelism is not airtight apologetics or motivational speaking. Rather, witnessing is showing others and telling them that we have seen the Risen Christ—in ourselves, in our world, and in whomever we're witnessing to. We bear witness to the love of Jesus Christ by being transparent, both in word and deed, about the manner in which grace, relinquishment, healing, purpose, and formative meaning in the midst of suffering is the bedrock of our spiritual life. Witnessing to Jesus is not a skill we develop, or a gift that only a few of us have. On the contrary, evangelism is the natural outgrowth and fruit of a grace-fueled, relinquished life and something that flows organically out of our experience of healing.

Witnessing is the work to which we are all called. And to do this work, quite frankly, we need to get more personal and vulnerable. Witnessing to the love and mercy of Jesus is not about describing God or motivating people to obey God, but rather about offering a personal word inside the chariot about the Son of God who loved you and gave himself for *you*.

Know Your Message

There is only one thing left to examine at this point about graceful evangelism. If we are to live our lives as witnesses to the mercy and grace of Jesus, it is not enough to know ourselves, other people, or even the Spirit of God at a deep level. We must also know our message. Being a witness is not just about showing, but also about telling. The Christian Gospel is a wonderful message of life-changing news that needs to be shared verbally. It wasn't Philip's demeanor or character that changed this eunuch's life. It was his message.

Going back to our story, this eunuch is on a spiritual wild goose chase. Everything he thought would make him happy—the power, the influence, and the money—they just haven't delivered. So he travels 1,600 miles to the Jewish temple. "Maybe I'll find God there," he thinks to himself. But when the eunuch arrives, he is barred from entry. "No one whose testicles are crushed or whose male organ is cut off shall enter the assembly of the Lord" (Deut. 23:1, ESV). This must have been a devastating and shameful experience. The Temple represented God's presence and the eunuch wasn't allowed to enter. He must have felt barred from the presence of God and too unclean or unfit to enter.

However, there is also a sense in which it is a good thing that the eunuch was barred from the Temple. After all, the Temple did not just represent God's presence, but also God's Law. The Temple was a symbol of moral purity. Those with clean hands and pure hearts were welcome, whereas sinners and those that did not keep the law were not welcome. People who had made themselves right with God through their own moral and ethical behavior and religious observance could enter God's presence, whereas the immoral could not enter the Temple.

The Romans may have destroyed the Jewish Temple in 70 CE, but what the Temple represents—*direct access to God through the merits of our own obedience, faithfulness, and moral striving*—is a philosophy that is alive and well. It is also a philosophy that adds much unneeded suffering and shame to human existence.

Metaphorically speaking, seeking God by going to the Temple is a dead end. Many people believe they will find God by trying harder to obey the Law. Some even think that when they start doing the deeds acceptable to God, God will accept them. That is *not* the Christian Gospel. In *New Clothes* I explain it like this:

> When most people imagine a "faithful Christian," they see a person committed above all else to an inner sense of duty that compels them to act morally superior to others. But if we read the gospels carefully, Jesus never appealed to our sense of duty, nor did he ever give a lecture on the importance of doing the right thing. In fact,

Jesus never said, "I am here to help you find God." Not once. What Jesus said was, "I am God. I am here to find you."[2]

This is the message of God's one-way love that lies at the heart of graceful evangelism. One-way love quite simply *is* our message. As Christians we have nothing to say about people's need to read their Bible, to stop sinning, or to clean up their act. Our message has nothing to do with a call to morality, and we offer no strategy on how people might get right with God. We simply smile and breathe and share the good news that, in and through Jesus Christ, God has already put things right between us and God's self and that nothing we do or don't do can ever change that.

Who's Chasing Whom?

The entire Bible is a story about a wild goose chase, not just Philip and the eunuch. If you and I are to witness to the love and mercy of Jesus, we have to get really clear on answering a very important question: Who's chasing whom?

I once heard a story about a retired greyhound racer that sheds some light on this question. This race dog had spent his entire life chasing a mechanical rabbit, and he had won lots of money for his owner and much fame for himself running competitively around a track.[3] But one day the dog decided to retire. This was confusing to all as the dog had won his last five races and had been so enthusiastic about his sport. No one understood why the greyhound quit racing, and so a reporter was sent to the dog's home to interview him.

"Why'd you quit," the reporter asked, "are you out of steam?" "No," replied the dog. "I still have some racing in me."

"Did they treat you badly or something?" The reporter thought this might be the reason, but alas it wasn't. "God no," said the dog. "They treated us like kings as long as we were winning."

"I see," said the reporter. "You must be injured?" "No," said the greyhound. "In fact, I am physically healthier and stronger than I've ever been."

"I don't understand," the reporter replied. "You were at the top of your game! Why would you quit racing at the height of your career?"

"I quit," the dog said, "the day I realized that what I was chasing was not a real rabbit. I spent so much of my life running, running, and running only to discover that the thing I was chasing *wasn't even real*."

This story unlocks the meaning of bearing witness to the grace and mercy of Jesus. We live in a world where just about everyone is caught up in some kind of spiritual wild goose chase. We're chasing after money, respect, control, fame, love, or perhaps to be a better Christian. We are all in our chariot chasing after something, and frankly, *we're exhausted*.

A witness to the grace and mercy of Jesus is someone that comes alongside people in their chariot and, when invited in, both shows and tells them the good news that God is actually the One chasing after them. The Gospel message that we have to share with the world is simply the story of God's outrageous wild goose chase to save us. It is wonderful news with a unique capacity to set the prisoners free and to open the eyes of the blind.

I wonder who in your life needs to hear that message. I wonder what aspects of your own heart have not yet been healed by the one-way love of God. Let the child within be reminded of this life-changing news that is so good that it's impossible not to share it.

Discussion Questions

1. How would you define "evangelism"? Have you ever shared your faith with someone? What was the experience like and what was the outcome?

2. What aspects of your character may prevent someone from inviting you "inside his or her chariot"?

3. What do you see as the role of the Holy Spirit in evangelism? How much of evangelism is our work? How much is God's work?

4. When it comes to being a witness, do you place more emphasis on our actions or our words? Why?

5. How would you define "personal language"? Why can it often feel risky to speak personal language? Do you have any relationships where speaking personal language comes naturally?

6. Has anyone ever tried to share his or her faith with you? What was that experience like?

7. How would you define "empathy"? How does empathy relate to the practice of evangelism?

7

Resurrection

"Now at last they were beginning Chapter One of the Great Story which no one on earth has read: which goes on forever: in which every chapter is better than the one before." —*C. S. Lewis*

"It's not the long walk home that will change this heart, but the welcome I receive with the restart." —*Mumford and Sons*

"A death must truly be a death before there can be a resurrection." —*David Zahl*

begin this final chapter with an embarrassing piece of self-disclosure. I am a hypochondriac. I interpret the tiniest bodily symptoms as a sure sign of impending death. In fact, I went through a two-year-stretch in seminary where I thought that every mole, spot, bump, headache, toothache, and dizzy spell was God's way of telling me that I had two months to live and that I needed to get my affairs in order.

The Internet and hypochondria don't go well together. In the last three years WebMD has diagnosed me with scoliosis, ADD, schizophrenia, polio, a serious neurological disorder, and four different types of cancer. Just yesterday I was moody and having hot flashes and the web doctor told me that I am in the early stages of menopause. My rational brain knows that the web doctor isn't accurate, but that doesn't change the fact that I sometimes feel like I am going to die.

Death makes us uncomfortable, afraid, lonely, and powerless. The thought of our inevitable demise is almost too much to bear, and so one might assume that the idea of resurrection offers us feelings of comfort, clarity, and power. But I find that the opposite is true, at least in part. I long for resurrection on the one hand, but I fear resurrection on the other.

The Living Dead

Our culture also simultaneously fears and welcomes resurrection. The proliferation of zombie movies like *Night of the Living Dead*, *Dawn of the Dead*, and *28 Days Later*, if nothing else, makes me think that when it comes to resurrection, the jury is still out. We both want resurrection and we fear it at the same time. Indeed there is something about the collective unconscious to produce such consistent scenes of mute and robotic dead people who still bear the semblance of life that reveals the ambivalence we feel about resurrection.

The Bible corroborates our fear of resurrection. When three women discovered the empty tomb on that first Easter morning, their instinctual response was to flee in fear: ". . . they said nothing to anyone, for they were afraid" (Mark 16:8).

I wonder if we fear resurrection because we often feel like zombies, the most common cultural image of resurrection that we are offered. A zombie is stuck in a "living death," which isn't a bad way of describing a life characterized by fear, scarcity, control, power, grasping, and suspicion—*our default, instinctual life*. This then becomes our dilemma: we fear death, and yet also fear the prospect of being trapped forever in a living death.

Unlikely Friends: Death and Resurrection

We fear resurrection because of resurrection's everlasting partnership, indeed *friendship*, with death. By death I don't just mean physical dying, but rather the experience of hitting rock bottom. We die whenever we reach that place where we know without a doubt that we have not an ounce of control. Death is the full and total relinquishment of our capacity to manufacture or control the outcome our ego desires.

Richard Rohr says that when we experience this beyond-control experience of death we come out the other side and that the word for this coming-out-the-other-side experience is "resurrection." "Something or someone seems to fill the tragic gap between death and life," he says, "but *only at the point of no return*."[1] The experience of resurrection is the epitome of relinquishment. No wonder we respond to resurrection like the women did on that first Easter morning. We keep our mouth shut about resurrection and we run away in fear.

Yet we find that we can't abandon our hope in resurrection. Our bones tell us that we are not meant to experience life as a living zombie. We hate the emptiness and stagnation that comes with a world fueled by competition, violence, and a suspicion of difference. Paul didn't have the zombie metaphor up his sleeve, but he routinely used the metaphor of sleepwalking to describe life as a living death. "The hour has come," he'd routinely say, "for you to wake from sleep" (Rom. 13:11, ESV).

Waking Up

Waking up is hard, which is why the experience of waking up is usually tied to the experience of suffering. Peter Senge tells the story of a Jamaican man named Fred who worked for the World Bank. Fred was diagnosed with a terminal disease. After accepting that he would only live a few more months, Fred ceased doing things he thought didn't matter. A terminal illness afforded Fred the opportunity to shed his sleepwalking patterns overnight. Fred stopped arguing with his mother, got involved in a program that served children, and refused to waste time getting upset over things he could not control.

One day Fred got a call from a doctor informing him that, in fact, his initial diagnosis had been wrong and that Fred actually had a rare form of a very curable disease. Upon hearing this news Fred broke down and began to cry like a baby, not because he was relieved, but rather because he was afraid that his life would return to the living death that it had formerly been. Fred didn't want to become a sleepwalker again. According to Senge, "It took a scenario that he was going to die for Fred to wake up."[2]

This is the irony of our condition: we fear death, and yet because we often experience life *as a living death* we are ambivalent about resurrection. The goal of the Christian life is to *die now* so that we can experience ourselves as already raised. Henry Nouwen shares:

> The death you fear is not simply the death at the end of your present life. Maybe the death at the end of your life won't be so fearful if you can die well now. Yes, the real death—the passage from time to eternity, from the transient beauty of this world to the lasting beauty of the next, from darkness into light—has to be made now.[3]

Resurrection is about the journey that Nouwen describes. Down, down, down we go, and at the point of no return we find ourselves waking up not to a living death but to eternal life—*now*.

Resurrection

Ambivalent as we may feel about the subject, resurrection simply is the hope that Christianity offers. Without a robust doctrine of resurrection, Christianity always slips into empty moralism. Paul bluntly puts it, "If Christ has not been raised, then our preaching is in vain and your faith is in vain" (1 Cor. 15:14, ESV).

My intention is not to offer an apologetic witness to the historicity of Jesus's bodily resurrection. I firmly believe that Jesus was raised bodily, and there are many fine books about the subject. This book just isn't one of them. Rather than asking whether Jesus could have resurrected in the past, I want to ask the much more difficult question: *Can we resurrect now?*

A Foreign World

Resurrection as a present experience is difficult to describe precisely because resurrection, *by definition*, is forever wed to foreignness and mystery. In fact, the more we experience resurrection, the more foreign and mysterious it becomes. This is the exact opposite of how every other human experience works. Other things become less foreign the more we experience them. For instance, the first time I took a yoga class I felt like an alien. I walked in late, didn't know where to put my mat, and I felt deeply intimidated by a roomful of people who all seemingly lacked vertebrae because they were twisted into a pretzel. When the instructor said "Namaste," I screamed "God bless you."

Yoga was an utterly foreign experience at first, but not anymore. Six weeks in, I stroll in like I own the place and unroll my mat onto *my* spot. I know the poses before they're announced, and I roll my eyes when someone's doing an up-dog when they should be in low-cobra. I no longer experience yoga as a foreign mystery because I have experienced so much of it. Resurrection as a present experience doesn't work like yoga or any other human experience.

There is no diminishing experience of foreignness and mystery the more we taste resurrection. The Risen Christ consistently meets us on our journey, but always in "another form" (Mark 16:12). Resurrection, it seems, is *another form* of experience altogether. Resurrection can feel scary and strange, namely because resurrection threatens whatever world we have constructed. Resurrection is a constant changing of forms, and only the relinquished, open, expectant, and waiting self can know resurrection.

Knowing Resurrection

We struggle to experience resurrection as a present reality because we try to access resurrection through a rational structure of consciousness. In the twenty-first century, as children of the Enlightenment, we have been trained to access truth in intellectual and deductive ways. We fail to appreciate sensory, intuitive, and subtle forms of knowing that transcend our rational consciousness.

This is problematic because resurrection as a present experience is never something we know with our rational mind. Our rational mind can make a strong case that Jesus *was* raised two thousand years ago, but to experience the Risen Christ now, *and ourselves as already raised in Him*, we must access "another form" of knowing.

Resurrection is like a radio that transmits FM waves. We quite simply cannot access resurrection with the AM tuner of our rational mind, which likes to categorize, control, and construct reality. Our AM tuner can understand elements of everything we have said thus far about grace, relinquishment, healing, purpose, suffering, and evangelism, but not resurrection. To know resurrection now we need a different structure of consciousness altogether, a different tuner so to speak. We need a way of knowing that includes rational thought while at the same time transcending rational thought. We cannot put the new wine of resurrection into the old wineskins of rationalism. It just won't work.

Another Form of Knowing

The Bible proves a faithful guide in helping us "know" resurrected reality. In fact, the Bible doesn't even have a word that captures our Western understanding of knowledge—a "knowledge" that analyzes and compartmentalizes the world as if we, the "knower," were disconnected and separate from whatever reality it is that we seek to "know."

The Hebrew word translated "know" is *yada*, a word that speaks to a deep, wordless, experiential, and even sexual form of knowing. *Yada* is not a knowing of the mind through a process of abstract conceptualization, but rather the deep experience of self as interpenetrated by the other. It is precisely this *yada* we must access. Whenever we reduce our experience of resurrection into a conceptual box, our words inevitably betray our experience. We find that the Risen Christ has moved on and that Jesus is dancing elsewhere in "another form."

Resurrection is not synonymous with an elevated consciousness. This is not some Jungian switcheroo. But I do contend that only an elevated consciousness knows, sees, tastes, and experiences resurrection as a present reality. I also believe that people with relatively undeveloped forms of cognitive capacity can know, see, and taste resurrection, such as children and people with mental handicaps. But for those of us who have eaten from the Tree of Knowledge and find that we are banished from Eden, "another form" of knowing is required. No longer can we seek to know resurrection in order that we might love it. Resurrection is always something we love in order to know.

The Present Future

In *Surprised by Hope*, N. T. Wright paints a gripping picture of a resurrected universe, and Wright argues that the future resurrection of all things is our ultimate biblical hope. The Christian hope is not that when we die we go to heaven, but rather how at the end of the age heaven will come to earth. Resurrection is first and foremost teleological and the future resurrection of all created things is the ultimate purpose for which God designed the universe. Resurrection, therefore, is chiefly something that happens at the end of time—a "future event" so to speak. The author of the Book of Revelation describes it in this way:

> I saw the holy city, new Jerusalem, coming down out of heaven from God, prepared as a bride adorned for her husband. And I heard a loud voice from the throne saying, "Behold, the dwelling place of God is with man. He will dwell with them, and they will be his people, and God himself will be with them as their God. He will wipe away every tear from their eyes, and death shall be no more, neither shall there be mourning, nor crying, nor pain anymore, for the former things have passed away." And he who was seated on the throne said, "Behold, I am making all things new." (Rev. 21:2–5)

We experience resurrection as a present reality when we first understand resurrection as a future event that has broken into our present experience. Resurrection *now* is like reverse time travel. It's not so much that we visit the future but that the future visits us. Resurrection is what God plans to do with the entire creation at the end of time. However, the transrational eye of faith can "know" that God's future resurrected reality has already broken into our present experience. We can taste, see, and experience resurrection *now*.

It is difficult to articulate how this might be so, and I candidly confess that I am an amateur on the subject. The map I have provided these past six chapters I know to be reliable and true. But in the pages that follow I offer no map, but rather the foggy directions of a bumbling traveler. Yes I describe a land that I have seen, but only as Paul says "as in a mirror dimly." I've been to the outskirts of the destination I describe, but I don't remember how I got there and to be honest I remember only a few of the details. What follows is a dim reflection of what I recall.

Resurrection Now

I recall that everything we do on this earth is meaningful, significant, and that *all things* in life—the good, the bad, and the ugly—will one day be redeemed and beautified and indeed that this has already been accomplished. Our bad and hateful actions and experiences will not be forgotten, but transformed and viewed for all eternity as *the good we always intended them to be*. Mistakes will not be forgotten, but transformed and viewed differently for all of eternity.

Consider the artist that takes a diverse set of elements like newspaper ads, movie tickets, and torn pieces of a magazine and then assembles them into a beautiful collage. This speaks to what God intends to do with every human being, and indeed with the human race, at the end of time. God will not weed out the mistakes, failure, and heartbreak and *then* make something beautiful out of the human race with what's leftover. Rather, that which we experience as "bad" now will be seen, felt, and revisited as much as we like through a much different lens: *as the good it was always meant to be*.

But what about all the evil in the world? It is a fair question, and I offer no easy answer. After all, the tragedy many experience in our world is unspeakable and we shudder to even think about the magnitude of human suffering. We prefer to think of resurrection as a restart. We expect God to throw out the tragedy, the mistakes, the failure, the misunderstandings, and the pain. We don't just want God to forgive. We prefer that God *forget*. There is so much we prefer to just forget about in our life as well.

I suppose that God could forget the atrocities and the evil and that resurrection could wipe them out so to speak. But if God did such a thing, consider: What would remain of your *actual life*, not to mention the history of the world? Can God really wipe out all evil without wiping out the story of struggling humanity?

I find Augustine helpful in pondering these matters. Augustine and most orthodox theologians have long insisted that evil does not exist as its own ontological category. Evil is that which is not. At root, evil is a deep perversion of things that are: the good, the beautiful, and the true.

I don't advocate for removing the word evil from our vocabulary, and it would be cruel to label things like the Holocaust and child abuse as good. Indeed, whatever good lies behind these heinous acts is so perverted that it would be disingenuous to say that we see any good behind these actions whatsoever. But consider a less heinous example of an act that we universally consider bad: robbery.

Bessel A. van der Kolk tells the story about a fourteen-year-old boy named Jack who had been arrested for breaking into his neighbor's house when they were away on vacation. The burglar alarm was sounding and the police found Jack in the living room, apparently in no hurry to exit the home. On Christmas Eve, van der Kolk was called in to interview Jack. He writes:

> The first question I asked Jack was who he expected would visit him in jail on Christmas. "Nobody," he told me. "Nobody ever pays attention to me." It turned out that he had been caught during break-ins numerous times before. He knew the police, and they knew him. With delight in his voice, he told me that when the cops saw him standing in the middle of the living room, they yelled, "Oh my God, it's Jack again, that little [jerk]." Somebody recognized him; somebody knew his name. A little while later Jack confessed, "You know, that is what makes it worthwhile." Kids will go to almost any length to feel seen and connected.[4]

There are two ways one can view Jack and his choice to break into his neighbor's home. The first is through the reductionist lens of right and wrong, good and bad, victim and perpetrator. Here Jack is clearly the perpetrator, and his neighbors are the victims. Jack is more wrong, flawed, and dysfunctional than his peers that aren't spending Christmas in jail. Perhaps we can picture Jack in the Kingdom of God one day, but assuming this incident is a microcosm of Jack's life, none of Jack's *actual experience* will be incorporated into that Kingdom. Very little of Jack will be included in God's great collage.

We can also know Jack in another form. We can see Jack's life and story through resurrection eyes. We can look at the good that Jack so desperately seeks—the good that has no doubt been denied Jack through a life of neglect and abandonment. All Jack wants, indeed all *any of us want,* is to be seen and to feel connected and valued, which are all good things that Jack seeks out in the only way he knows how. *It is not all Jack's fault.* Not that we blame Jack's parents for his behavior. Like Jack, they too are both perpetrator and victim, and as such they're also caught seeking the good in the most perverse sort of way with the rest of the human race.

Life as an Overflowing Hand

Jack's story illustrates a very important truth; we see and experience life differently as we know life in another form—through resurrection eyes. We know that *all of Jack*—the good, the bad, the ugly—will be part of God's beautiful, eternal collage where all things participate in creating the good that was always meant to be.

If this is true, the question then becomes: what does it mean to "know" God's future resurrection as *already* present with us now? To answer this question, we return to an image from chapter two: Robert Capon's "the dead hand." I quote him again to remind you of his thinking.

> I want you to hold out your right hand, palm up, and imagine that someone is placing, one after another, all sorts of good gifts in it. Make the good things whatever you like—M&M's, weekends in Acapulco, winning the lottery, falling in love, having perfect children, being wise, talented, good-looking, and humble besides—anything. But now consider. There are two ways your hand can respond to those goods. It can respond to them as a live hand and try to clutch,

to hold onto the single good that is in it at any given moment—thus closing itself to all other possible goods, or it can respond as a dead hand—in which case it will simply lie there perpetually open to all the goods in the comings and goings of their dance.[5]

We can view Capon's image in two different ways. The first would be to call it a *dead hand*—a metaphor that we have already explored at length. However, we can also see *an overflowing hand*.

This simply *is* the paradox of the Christian life. *Only a dead hand can overflow with life.* We fall into grace and come out the other side resurrected. The life of grace whereby we relinquish control, find healing, discover our purpose, find meaning in the midst of our suffering, and bear witness to Christ in the midst of that experience isn't a prelude to resurrection—it *is* resurrection *now*. It is an overflowing life of grace through and through whereby we let go of everything only to find that we have possessed all things from the beginning. We need to let go of our need to label Jack as a troublemaker, or interpret our suffering as a sign of God's absence. We let go of our need to clutch altogether. Our hand dies, and in the midst of that dying experience we come to know the dead hand as raised and overflowing.

Resurrection *now* is life as an overflowing hand. The fruit of this life is seen in our deep desire to (1) contextualize our wounds, (2) amplify our sense of community, and (3) live a life of refused violence.

Contextualizing Our Wounds

The experience of resurrection empowers us to contextualize our wounds. We increasingly come to see all of our pain and wounds in the context of Easter. We know that Jesus has made all things new, even the deepest wounds that we have suffered.

This is not to say that we devalue our wounds. Rather we refuse to elevate our story of wounding over somebody else's story of wounding.

We refuse to get lost in the world's mad frenzy of ressentiment. We don't huddle in groups where everyone has a similar story of pain and then caucus with them in an effort to coerce people with lesser wounds to take responsibility for our pain. On the contrary, we take responsibility for our life and story and believe that the crucified Christ reigns in the midst of our story of pain. We believe that Jesus has turned our wounds into our finest trophy, and indeed have even experienced this to be true.

This process of contextualizing our wounds is deeply personal, and yet paradoxically we cannot do it alone. We need empathetic others who can listen to our story and help us make meaning out of our wounds in such a way that we do not see ourselves as victims, but rather as agents and actors in Jesus's work here on earth.

Only in the context of a community filled with grace can we shift our focus from our wounds to the beautiful collage that God is weaving together from every human life. In community we understand that our wounding is mystically bound up with the resolution of Easter. Seeing that the resurrected Christ retained his wounds, this strengthens our resolve to let our wounds flow in and out of the open-faced hand that has become our resurrected life.

This of course completely changes how we relate to other people, not to mention how they experience us. No longer do we view people through our wounds. People cease to be walking symbols that we instinctively categorize as "like me" or "not like me." We now know every human being to be a walking and wounded miracle—an indispensable part of God's final masterpiece.

The openhanded life of grace always contextualizes our wounds. Like running water softens stone, seeing the flow of grace in all of our circumstances softens how we experience others. We know that in Christ every human life is bound up with our own and that any "me" that exists apart from "you" is an illusion.

Being as Communion

The resurrected life is a deeply interdependent life. It may be natural and developmentally appropriate to grow up imagining that we exist as a separate self with a capacity to connect or not connect with other people. However, seeing life through resurrected eyes, we come to know ourselves *primarily* as a bundle of interconnected and enmeshed relationships with a capacity to become, or perhaps discover, that we are also a distinct self. We are distinct from everyone else, but disconnected from no one.

In South Africa they call this "Ubuntu," which loosely translated means "my humanity is bound up with yours." The "we" is always present in the "I." We are not so much self-made individuals as we are a bundle of potential that will manifest only in relationship. "I" always manifests differently depending on the relationship.

Paul once noted that when one member of the Body of Christ suffers we all suffer. When we experience life as an overflowing hand, Paul's assertion becomes crystal clear. As we look at life through resurrected eyes, it becomes increasingly difficult to see myself apart from my connection with all of humanity. There is no person past, present, or future that I am not enmeshed with.

Albert Einstein called our feelings of separateness an optical delusion of consciousness. The delusion of separateness always leaves us imprisoned and stuck in a small world of petty personal desires where our affection is limited to a small number of people. In a culture built on individualism, few of us want to see how enmeshed and interconnected we are. Seeing our interconnectedness would force us to take responsibility for how our thoughts and behaviors impact everyone else. It would mean seeing that a person is a person only through other people.

Our deep entanglement ceases to be a burden when we live life as an overflowing hand. Indeed quite the opposite. As I see my deep interconnection with everyone else, I realize that there is no such thing as an expendable human being. *Everyone else must exist for me to be "me."* My life just doesn't make sense as an integral part of God's great collage if everyone else's life—that I have created and that has in turn created me—is not present as well.

Seeing our deep entanglement is what enables us to contextualize our wounds in the first place. We discover that there is nothing inside of me that doesn't also exist in you and that the deep impulses behind both the best and the worst of human behavior reside within us all. Maya Angelou was raped as a teenager, and she tells a powerful story of how she learned to forgive her rapist. "Eventually I had to realize that I was my rapist," she said, "that the anger that was in him is in me as well."[6]

Some might experience Angelou's statement as offensive, and indeed only a woman with her profile can get away with saying such a thing. We prefer to see rapists as monsters—nonhuman *others* from whom we can disassociate. However, resurrection eyes see how each person is made of connections to every other person. No one's uniqueness is any more valuable than anyone else's. Some of us may be more damaged than others, but each human being is an integral part of God's great collage, and even the worst atrocities, which the human race creates collectively, are forgiven by God ahead of time. They are accounted for, known, and in the end will be flipped upside down in a way that will increase our eternal sense of joy and connection. It is this knowledge that creates a life of nonviolence.

A Life of Refused Violence

The surest sign that we are living life as an open and overflowing hand is that our heart refuses to engage in violence and coercion. Violence is always a failure to relinquish. Violence happens naturally when our hands are clutched.

Much of our violence stems from the myth that sees time as a scarce resource. We assume that the clock of life is ticking, that good things are limited, and that we would be a fool not to grab our share of the pie while we still can. We forget that resurrection is an eternity of time and that to God a thousand years and a day are one in the same.

Our default state is to experience time as fleeting, and if we are honest, most of our moments are just wasted. We lack the capacity to fully experience every moment of every day. Just recall what you remember from this time last week. You may recall something especially negative that happened, or looking at your calendar may jog your memory a bit, but I imagine that the vast majority of what you were doing at this time last week is *dead*. Only a few experiences actually turn into a memory, and even memories fade and change over time.

In God's future Kingdom we will have infinite and endless time to revisit this life—the very life you experience now as you read these words, the life you assumed you'd leave behind one day for some better and wound-free heavenly existence. We will one day awaken in God's great mosaic and have the opportunity to explore every moment of our life for all of eternity in light of grace. There is no resource *less scarce* than time. The resurrection will afford you the opportunity to explore all of your life in the light of God's grace.

This includes the hurtful moments you prefer stay buried. *In the Kingdom of God, nothing stays buried.* Everything is dug up and exposed and presented "in another form" for all of eternity. The mean words, the neglect, the untimely illness, the miscarriage, the struggle to find love, the divorce, and your friend's suicide—you will explore all of these for eternity hand in hand with everyone else and see them much differently. You will see in these things that caused you so much pain not the evil you assumed they were *but the good they were always meant to be and can now only exist as for all of eternity.*

We find ourselves in the midst of eternity *now*. Everything is everywhere already healed and reconciled and seen by God as the good it was always meant to be and forever is. Time is not a scarce resource. There is an eternity of time and we find ourselves amidst that eternity now.

Knowing this to be true allows us to relax. We find that we can slow down, relax, and revel in the ordinary moments of life, which makes for a less violent existence. Thomas Merton shares:

> There is a pervasive form of contemporary violence to which the idealist most easily succumbs: activism and overwork. The rush and pressure of modern life are a form, perhaps the most common form, of its innate violence. To allow oneself to be carried away by a multitude of conflicting concerns, to surrender to too many demands, to commit oneself to too many projects, to want to help everyone in everything, is to succumb to violence. The frenzy of our activism neutralizes our work for peace. It destroys our own inner capacity for peace. It destroys the fruitfulness of our own work, because it kills the root of inner wisdom which makes work fruitful.[7]

There is something about seeing God's eternity of time that enables us to relax. We come to understand that fruitfulness in life is not about accomplishing big things, but about acquiring a big heart. Mother Theresa was once asked what enabled her to accomplish such great things in her life. "You cannot do great things," she replied. "You can only do small things with great love."[8] This simply is a life of refused violence. It is a life that is small, patient, humble, hidden, transparent, and relinquished to God through and through—a life that we can explore in depth because we know that we have an eternity to do it.

The Undoing of the Fall

The core myth that often explains humanity's separation and isolation is called "the Fall." We recall that Adam and Eve's Fall was primarily an alteration of knowledge. After all, the forbidden fruit was taken from "The Tree of the Knowledge of Good and Evil." Before they ate from this tree, Adam and Eve knew that they were deeply connected to God, each other, and creation. However, after eating from this tree, their knowledge was altered. They knew separateness, violence, and a suspicion of difference—a living death.

If the Fall involved an alteration of knowledge, it makes sense that resurrection is ultimately *a second alteration of knowledge*. We return to "another form" of knowing. We come to know our wounds as part of God's great collage, ourselves as deeply connected with every human being, and a life of nonviolence through the openhanded life of grace. Above all else we come to know that humanity never fell *from* grace. We fell *into* grace. Indeed every second of human existence has been a falling into grace from the start, a reality that we have hitherto been blind to.

Re-Membering

Richard Rohr tells a great story about a young couple on their first night at home with their second child. They had just left the hospital and the moment they put the baby down for the night, their four-year-old son said to them, very calmly, "If you don't mind, I'd like to talk to my brother." The parents replied, "Well of course, you can talk to the baby whenever you want, but it's bedtime now." But the little boy pressed: "No, I want to talk to my brother now, it's important; and the two of us need to be alone." And so surprised and a little curious, the parents let the little boy into the nursery and cupped their ears to the door wondering what on earth he might say, and this is what they heard: "Quick! Tell me where you came from. Quick! Tell me who made you." And then the boy said this. "Please, tell me. I am beginning to forget."[9]

My deep hope is that I have sparked your desire to remember what is and has always been true about you and about everyone else you love: We are all reconciled to one another and to God *now*. As Julian of Norwich put it, "It was necessary that there should be sin; but all shall be well, and all shall be well, and all manner of things shall be well."

Jesus's way of descent is not about us making things well through our own effort, ingenuity, and cleverness—we do not ascend to wellness. Rather we descend deep into ourselves to find the Living Christ, and in the process we experience a deep remembering that *re*-members us. We see that there is no need to fear resurrection and that death is always a falling into grace.

Discussion Questions

1. Do you see resurrection more as a future event or as a present experience? Is it possible to experience resurrection *now*? Why or why not?

2. Is there a part of you that fears resurrection? Is so, why? If not, why not?

3. Is it possible to "know" something in a way that reason alone can't explain? Have you ever known something in this "transrational" sort of way before?

4. When the Kingdom of God arrives in its fullness, do you think the pain, tragedy, and heartbreak of our lives will be completely forgotten? Why or why not?

5. What does it mean to contextualize our wounds? Do you believe that some people's wounds deserve more attention that others? Why or why not?

6. What does it mean to live life as an "overflowing hand"? Can you think of a time in your life when you experienced life in this way?

7. Do you believe that you are deeply connected to every person on this planet? Can you imagine yourself existing without others? Why or why not?

Endnotes

Introduction

1. I borrow this story from Eckhart Tolle, *The Power of Now: A Guide to Spiritual Enlightenment* (Novato, CA: Namaste Publishing, 1999), 11.

2. I borrow this story from Mark Elliot's reflection on the "homiletical perspective" of 2 Corinthians 4:13—5:1 in *Feasting on the Word: Year B, Volume 3*, edited David L. Bartlett and Barbara Brown Taylor (Louisville: Westminster John Knox Press, 2009), 115.

Chapter 1

1. The term "moralistic therapeutic deism" made its debut in *Soul Searching: The Religious and Spiritual Lives of American Teenagers* by Christian Smith and Melinda Lundquist Denton (New York: Oxford University Press, 2005).

2. See Matthew 20:16 for Jesus's thoughts on the matter.

3. James Bryan Smith, *The Good and Beautiful God: Falling in Love with the God Jesus Knows* (Downers Grove, IL: InterVarsity Press, 2009), 41.

4. Brennan Manning, *The Ragamuffin Gospel* (Sisters, OR: Multnomah, 2000), 22. Italics mine.

5. I was introduced to Kolbe's story by my tour guide at Auschwitz. I have since heard other preachers tell his story as an illustration. For more information on Kolbe's life, I suggest the following: "Maximilian Kolbe" *Wikipedia*. Wikimedia Foundation, 01 Nov. 2014. Web. 12 Jan. 2014. It is worth noting that the man Kolbe substituted himself for survived his time at Auschwitz.

6. Thomas Merton, *No Man Is an Island* (New York: Hartcourt, 1955), 241.

7. Paul F. M. Zahl, *Grace in Practice: A Theology of Everyday Life* (Grand Rapids, MI: Wm. B. Eerdmans, 2007), 76.

8. Ibid., 36.

9. Robert Farrar Capon, *Between Noon and Three: Romance, Law, and the Outrage of Grace* (Grand Rapids, MI: Wm. B. Eerdmans, 1997), 74.

10. My wife's editorial comments here were, "So you wrote a book?" Clearly I am still working on my need to accomplish less.

11. Thomas Merton, *New Seeds of Contemplation* (New York: New Directions, 2007), 61–62.

12. Ibid., 62.

13. Robert Farrar Capon, *Kingdom, Grace, Judgment: Paradox, Outrage, and Vindication in the Parables of Jesus* (Grand Rapids, MI: Wm. B. Eerdmans, 2002), 252–53.

14. See Ephesians 1. Notice that all of the verbs are in the past tense. Our salvation and adoption is 100 percent complete. We simply need to *wake up* to that wonderful truth.

15. Merton, *New Seeds of Contemplation*, 74–75.

16. Thomas Merton, *Thoughts in Solitude* (New York: Farrar, Straus & Cudahy, 1958), 3.

17. I have not actually read Edwards's sermon on Job, but learned this from Peter Scazzero's *Emotionally Healthy Spirituality: Unleash a Revolution in Your Life in Christ* (Nashville, TN: Thomas Nelson, 2006), 136.

18. Merton, *Thoughts in Solitude*, 25–26.

19. Henri J. M. Nouwen, *Reaching Out: The Three Movements of the Spiritual Life* (Garden City, NY: Doubleday, 1975), 118–19.

Chapter 2

1. Merton, *New Seeds of Contemplation*, 47.

2. You may wish to delve more into human psycho/social development from the works of Sigmund Freud, Erik Erikson, or others as this is beyond the scope of this book.

3. Thomas Keating, *Invitation to Love: The Way of Christian Contemplation* (New York: Continuum, 1998), 8.

4. Held at Camp Allen, Navasota, Texas, in June of 2012, this conference was hosted by the Center for the Study of Natural Systems and the Family, http://csnsf.org/. Michael Kerr was the keynote speaker.

5. David G. Benner, *Spirituality and the Awakening Self: The Sacred Journey of Transformation* (Grand Rapids, MI: Brazos, 2012), 66.

6. Scazzero, *Emotionally Healthy Spirituality*, 127–32.

7. Eugene Peterson, *The Contemplative Pastor: Returning to the Art of Spiritual Direction* (Grand Rapids, MI: Wm. B. Eerdmans, 1993), 98.

8. See Ibid., 102–09. Much of this section borrows and builds on Peterson's work in these pages.

9. Ibid., 104–05.

10. Capon, *Grace, Kingdom, Judgment*, 256.

11. Richard J. Foster, *Prayer: Finding the Heart's True Home* (New York: HarperOne, 1992), 49.

12. Ibid., 49.

13. Ibid., 54–55.

Chapter 3

1. Benner, *Spirituality and the Awakening Self*, 82.

2. Brené Brown, *Daring Greatly: How the Courage to Be Vulnerable Transforms the Way We Live, Love, Parent, and Lead* (New York: Gotham, 2012), 112.

3. Yes my fellow Bible enthusiast, I have read Ephesians 6 and I hold it to be true. But please take note of the paradox Paul makes us contemplate. The "armor" of God is truth, righteousness, salvation, faith, and hope. Or as I interpreted these things in chapter one, we put on God's paradoxical armor as we see the cross, accept acceptance, and wait in weakness.

4. Glen A. Scorgie, *A Little Guide to Christian Spirituality* (Grand Rapids, MI: Zondervan, 2007), 90.

5. Michael E. Kerr and Murray Bowen, *Family Evaluation: An Approach Based on Bowen Theory* (New York: Norton, 1988), 18.

6. Foster, *Prayer*, 28. I rely heavily on Foster's chapter "The Prayer of Examen."

7. Ibid., 31.

8. I borrow this quote from John Ortberg's *Everybody's Normal Till You Get to Know Them* (Grand Rapids, MI: Zondervan, 2014), 13.

9. Larry Crabb, *Becoming a True Spiritual Community* (Nashville, TN: Thomas Nelson, 2007), 11.

10. Ibid., 27.

11. Ibid., 16.

12. Henri J. M. Nouwen, *The Wounded Healer: Ministry in Contemporary Society* (New York: Doubleday, 1979), 20.

Chapter 4

1. *http://babyublog.com/*

2. I borrow the word "wholehearted" from Brené Brown, *The Gifts of Imperfection: Let Go of Who You Think You're Supposed to Be and Embrace Who You Are* (Center City, MN: Hazelden, 2010).

3. Merton, *New Seeds of Contemplation*, 99.

4. Thomas Merton, *Seven Storey Mountain* (New York: Hartcourt, 1948), 256.

5. For Nietzsche there was also a political element to ressentiment. Perhaps Nietzsche only viewed purpose and causes through the lens of politics, or perhaps most causes gravitate towards the political arena when fueled by anger.

6. James Davison Hunter, *To Change the World: The Irony, Tragedy, and Possibility of Christianity in the Late Modern World* (New York: Oxford University Press, 2010), 107.

7. Nouwen, *The Wounded Healer*, 81–82.

8. Brennan Manning, *Ruthless Trust: The Ragamuffin's Path to God* (New York: HarperCollins, 2009).

Chapter 5

1. Timothy Keller, *Walking with God Through Pain and Suffering* (New York: Riverhead Books, 2013), 49.

2. Richard Rohr, *Falling Upward: A Spirituality for the Two Halves of Life* (San Francisco: Jossey-Bass, 2011), 73.

3. This particular talk was given at a national *Renovare* conference in April 2014 in Houston, TX.

4. Rohr, *Falling Upward*, 34.

5. Merton, *Spirituality and the Awakening Self*, 103.

6. Thomas E. Joiner, *Lonely at the Top: The High Cost of Men's Success* (New York: Macmillan, 2011), 91.

7. I suppose that for some, this experience of descent happens in an instant. That is not my experience. This descent into our own depths is something I experience as a process. I have experienced enough of what I am writing about to know that there is truth in what I say and that this map I offer, though simplistic, is reliable. However, I don't want to leave you with the impression that I have arrived, and I hope that if I made such a claim it would instantly disqualify me as anyone with a clue as to what constituted spiritual reality.

8. Rohr, *Falling Upward*, 73.

9. This is a mysterious verse and I reference it without a full rational grasp of what Paul means in saying it. I don't believe Paul is saying that Jesus's work on the cross is insufficient. I do think, however, that Paul is suggesting that on the Day of Resurrection God has ordained that all of our suffering, when taken as grace, will be part of the Grand Masterpiece Jesus called "the renewal of all things" (Matt 19:28). God will use our suffering for eternal and good purposes.

10. John W. Kleinig, "Oratio, Meditatio, Tentatio: What Makes a Theologian?" *Concordia Theological Quarterly* 66:3 (2002), 255–67. *www.johnkleinig.com/files/ 1813/2730/7611/Oratio_Meditatio_Tentatio.pdf*

11. Rohr, *Falling Upward*, 160.

12. Merton, *New Seeds of Contemplation*, 161.

Chapter 6

1. Peterson, *The Contemplative Pastor*, 62–63.

2. John Newton, *New Clothes: Putting on Christ and Finding Ourselves* (New York: Morehouse, 2014), 181.

3. I have modified this fable a bit, hearing it from a sermon given by Katherine Grieb at Virginia Theological Seminary in 2006. She attributed the story to Fred Craddock.

Chapter 7

1. Richard Rohr, *Immortal Diamond: The Search for Our True Self* (San Francisco: Jossey-Bass, 2013), xxi.

2. Peter M. Senge, *Presence: Human Purpose and the Field of the Future* (Cambridge, MA: SoL, 2004), 25–26.

3. Henri J. M. Nouwen, *The Inner Voice of Love: A Journey Through Anguish to Freedom* (New York: Doubleday, 1998), 107.

4. Bessel A. van der Kolk, *The Body Keeps the Score: Brain, Mind, and Body in the Healing of Trauma* (New York: Viking Press, 2014), 115.

5. Capon, *Grace, Kingdom, Judgment*, 256.

6. Senge, *Presence*, 126.

7. Thomas Merton, *Conjectures of a Guilty Bystander* (New York: Random House, 1968), 73.

8. Senge, *Presence*, 139.

9. Rohr, *Immortal Diamond*, xxi.